Mission and the Emerging Indian Middle Class

Papers of the 18th Annual Consultation
of Centre for Mission Studies (January 18-20, 2012)
held at Union Biblical Seminary, Pune

Mission and the Emerging Indian Middle Class

*Papers of the 18th Annual Consultation
of Centre for Mission Studies January 18-20, 2012
held at Union Biblical Seminary, Pune*

Editors

Sungjemmeren Kijong Imchen

&

Asangla Lemtur

CMS/UBS

2020

Cover Image: Akhriezo Shuya

ISBN: 978-93-88945-68-4

Laser typeset by

ISPCK, Post Box 1585, 1654, Madarsa Road, Kashmere Gate, Delhi-110006
• *Tel:* 23866323/22

e-mail: ashish@ispck.org.in • ella@ispck.org.in
website: www.ispck.org.in

Contents

Foreword - 1

UBS engages on the matters related to contemporary issues with scholars, researchers, theologians, activists, pastors, missionaries, social workers and churches during the CMS consultation. The CMS consultation of 2012 focused on the issues related to the "middle class". Unfortunately, our society including the Church is divided into different classes which is based on different criteria. However, the Bible envisions a classless society- the kingdom of God where justice, righteousness and equality reigns. Most of the problems in our world today are stemmed from stratification and hierarchy. Even in the so called "classless societies", two classes are evident: rich and the poor. These are further classified as super rich, rich, upper middle class, the middle class and the lower middle class and the poor. The most influential class among these is the "middle class". Economists opine that the recent economic crises in India is the outcome of "middle income trap". There is a debate whether we are already in the middle-income trap or will fall into it. The economic growth of India was based upon the consumption by 100 million middle class people who were at the top of socio-economic pyramid. According to some, the consumption by this group has reached a stage of saturation which is causing a decline in demand. Thus, slowing down the economy which is resulting in loss of jobs in the whole country in all sectors. The present economic crises in India makes us to understand how the middle class can impact the whole society and economy of a nation.

The articles in this book deals with socio-economic, religious and spiritual issues related to the middle class in India. The data and research published in this book will help churches, organisations and individuals to interact with the middle class and serve them more effectively. I congratulate the organisers of the consultation and the editors of the book for arranging the consultation and publishing this book for the use of Church and society.

Praveen Paul, D. Th.
Principal, Union Biblical Seminary

Foreword - 2

I consider it a privilege to write this Foreword! It is a matter of joy that Interserve could initiate the "Survey Research on Serving Middle Class Indians" with a purpose of understanding and strategizing to share the Good News with people of other faith and contribute to mission research. I am happy that these research findings along with other reflective papers presented during the consultation on the topic have come out as a book!

The project assumes significance as the urban middle class is the fastest growing segment and they need the Good News like any other people group which lives in remote corners of this land.

I can see the sincere efforts put in by the personnel to collect reliable data to get the best results. As the survey has covered 7 important cities from all four directions of India, the findings will enable churches and organisations to develop skill sets and approaches to reach them. I do hope that the research findings will help the churches, organisations and mission practitioners to understand the beliefs and convictions of the middle class about God, religion, perception of salvation, prayers, etc.

I also believe that these findings will also enable our churches and agencies to encourage and engage suitable personnel to address the needs of the urban middle class and communicate the love of Christ in the most appropriate ways.

As we see major transitions in the socio-political and religious scenario in our country and elsewhere, this book comes out at the right time as a spark to ignite fruitful discussions and further research.

On behalf of Interserve India, I thank Union Biblical Seminary for its efforts to publish this as a book. Our special thanks to John Amalraj, my predecessor and Lunkhomang Haokip, former Research Coordinator of Interserve for their hard work in spearheading this research

Arul Manohar, Ph.D.
Executive Secretary & National Director
Interserve India

Preface

Why the Middle Class? The simple answer is that Jesus loves all segments of society. While studying and teaching Church Growth through the years with a special interest in India, it became evident that many early mission pioneers had an intention to reach those in more powerful positions in society. What happened in fact was that the influence among the higher strata was limited and the response of more marginalized populations was promising. The larger movements to Christ in the early days of missions in India happened in the lower levels of society. This was due in part to the spiritual and social betterment that Christianity offered to the marginalized. Take for example the interesting case of Roberto De Nobili who was an early master of language and contextual style among the elite, and yet his remarkable work among the upper class was finally very limited in scope. Realizing that the work of his missionary peers was identified with the bad habits of other foreigners, he sought to identify with the purer lifestyle of the societal elite. The hope for a trickle-down effect which would influence all of society was only partially realized.

It was only natural for expatriates, like William Carey, who came into Indian society under the auspices of powerful institutions such as the British East India Company, to enjoy the shelter and opportunities that powerful alignments offered. Carey might not have had the opportunity and financial base to pursue his vision in India at that time if it were not for his connection with this foreign institution. We understand that these early missioners left behind many things in order to follow their calling into what were in those days uncharted situations. We stand on the shoulders of these pacesetters who gave up and risked much to move out into the unknown to proclaim the good news among unreached populations. And yes Carey, like Daniel the Prophet and Joseph the Administrator, leveraged the power of the palace in the hope that all levels of society would be influenced. Carey's model, though limited in effect among the larger society, was foundational for what would come later.

Early mission efforts were met with limited receptivity in the rocky soil of the privileged of Indian society. Eventually, the most fruitful responses were found among the disenfranchised scheduled castes and scheduled tribes. The history of mission in India actually shows that whereas work among the elite was interesting and well-intentioned, the walls between societal groups limited the flow of the gospel. When the upper castes were resistant, ministry efforts shifted focus from upper society to lower society where it met with remarkable receptivity. Some of these groups would experience wonderful stories of what Donald McGavran called "redemption and lift," whereby they would find spiritual life in Christ and accompanying growth in economic and social power. While the Church continues to expand among these marginal peoples, sadly many still struggle to realize significant social lift and are kept in the margins. What in fact happened, with a few exceptions, is that mission aimed at the upper and lower levels of Indian society and largely ignored the middle strata. In some sense mission had largely become associated with the poor in slums and rural villages. Some of these found that Christianity allowed them to move upward into the middle class. Modern sensitivities among missioners has awakened some interest in doing justice among those who have been overlooked in the sharing of gospel opportunities.

This collection of papers is a noble attempt to stir interest and formulate strategy toward this prospect. In fact there are many success stories in India among the middle class, but there is still much work to be done if the love of Christ is to be properly represented to these who have some security and position in life but are empty within. Our special thanks to the leadership of Interseve India who sponsored an excellent piece of research into the Indian middle class forming the core around which this consultation and the resulting papers were shaped. Thanks also to the faculty friends at Union Biblical Seminary who have prompted and polished these papers. Now it remains for us to be spiritually sensitive and intentional as to the distribution and equity of mission efforts in the years ahead. Jesus loves the middle class and we should love them in word and deed.

Frampton F. Fox, D.Min., Ph.D.
Professor of Global Studies
Liberty University

Introduction

The 18th Centre for Mission Studies Annual Consultation was held from January 18-20, 2012. Frampton F. Fox and Sungjemmeren K. Imchen were the coordinators. "Mission and the Emerging Middle Class" was its theme, which has been adopted as the title of this book. It is a collection of edited papers of this consultation. Nine papers were presented but only five have made it to this book.

Interserve and Union Biblical Seminary signed a Memorandum of Understanding and jointly sponsored this consultation. This CMS consultation was centred on an empirical research conducted by the Interserve in some major Indian cities. The findings of this research have formed the first chapter, "Survey Research on Serving middle-class Indians: A Project of Interserve India". In this chapter, John Amalraj and Lunkhomang Haokip, evaluatively describe the Middle Class Indians in terms of their spiritual change and suggest strategies to reach out to them.

The second chapter, "The Middle Class in India and Some Lessons from the Bible on Reaching Them" by J. N. Manokaran can be divided into two major parts. Firstly, the emergence of and the challenges of the Middle Class in India; Secondly, a biblical basis for reaching them, in which he uses the example of fifteen well-to-do people of the Bible.

The third chapter, "Contemporary Middle Class Youth in India: Challenges and Opportunities for the Church" by John M Prasad describes the emerging middle class youth in India and presents four strategies for reaching them.

The fourth chapter, "TEE Helps to Enable Christian Engagement with the Indian Middle Classes" by Eric Clouston discusses the emergence of the Indian middle class; exposes some examples of Christian engagement; and proposes some ways for the church in India to respond to the challenges of the Indian middle class.

The fifth chapter, "An Interview with a Member of US Middle Class and Possible Implication for Ministry" by Vicki Brown is a comparative analysis of the middle class in the United States and India. She narrates a story of a 'lower-upper' middle class family in the US out of which she construes servanthood as evangelistic tool.

There has been a gap of more than eight years between the consultation in 2012 and publication of this book. This publication was made possible by the Research and Publication Committee of Union Biblical Seminary who resolved to edit and publish CMS consultation papers along with the coordinator of a consultation. For that we are thankful to the Research and Publication Committee members of UBS. Our sincere thanks go to Praveen Paul (Principal, UBS) for writing the Foreword, Frampton F. Fox (one of the coordinators of the consultation) for writing the preface and John Amalraj (former Director of Interserve) for his patience and constant encouragements.

Finally, we want to express our warm appreciation to all the paper presenters whose essays have made it and sincere apologies to those whose essays could not.

Sungjemmeren Kijong Imchen
&
Asangla Lemtur

Survey Research on Serving Middle Class Indians: A Project of Interserve India

John Amalraj and Lunkhomang Haokip***

"Mobilizing the churches to share the Good News among middle class Indians of other faiths" – John Amalraj

Introduction

This survey research addresses the issue of how middle class Indians of other faiths, who are thinkers and movers of the society, could be reached with the gospel in their context. The survey aims to develop contextually appropriate approaches of sharing the Good News among middle class Indians. The primary information used in this survey research is on socio-religious perspectives of other faiths concerning their knowledge, attitudes and practices to develop possible ways of making Christ known to them personally. This survey was undertaken among selected major cities of India: Bangalore, Kolkata, Nagpur, Pune, Chennai, Ahmedabad and Guwahati. These cities are chosen as they were considered vital economical, cultural and political centers and Information Technology hub of the country among others. A standardized and validated study questionnaire was developed as a tool to survey the cities with uniform methodology. The questionnaire dealt with questions on how best the churches and mission agencies would be able to serve the middle Class segment of the country with the love of God.

Based on this socio-religious survey data on other faiths, the survey came to a conclusion that majority of the study population think positively towards Christians. The time when other faiths considered Christians as western culture followers or foreigners was fast diminishing. Hence, developing a contextual approach in reaching the middle class is the need of the hour. The following perspectives were taken into consideration in this survey: What they know, attitude and practices concerning God, Sin, Salvation, Prayer, Jesus, Christians, Religions, Personal life, Family life, Christian role and Middle Class of other faiths becoming the follower of Christ. These factors will help the churches, mission agencies and any other mission practitioners, providing them a solid tool as they engage in serving the middle-class Indians with the kingdom message.

The Research Problem and Method

Statement of the Problem

The Churches and mission agencies have been ministering mainly among the poor, rural and tribal backgrounds; hence in many instances the middle class population which is dynamically growing has been neglected. This study proposes to address this growing need by studying the socio-religious views of the middle class Indians.

Elaboration of the Problem

The Indian economy is controlled by the 'purchasing power' of the middle mlass. This segment of middle class Indians around 300 million people, are equivalent to the total population of USA. Manokaran asserted, "The middle and the upper classes are the educated, articulate, opinion formers, trendsetters and decision-makers of the society. They control the economic, social and political power structure of the country. Since these powerful classes have not heard the gospel, there is no transformation for good in this nation."[1] The projected population ratio of India's middle income families (above ₹90,000 a year) was 48.4% in the year 2009, up from the current 28%. They are the basis for public opinion that influences government decisions and target of multinational businesses. Rajendran lamented, "some work is done among the poor, but very little work among the powerful middle class consumers."[2] Unfortunately, with the ethos of "win the winnable while they can be won," strategic people groups like the middle class are neglected.

The church and missions in general are not well-equipped to reach the urban upper and middle class people. Most Christian workers are trained to either go to remote rural places or become pastors of the existing Christian community. Very little pioneering work is done on urban middle class people and there are very few models available to follow.

Who are the Middle Class Indians?

The term 'middle class' is a conglomeration of several classes and is defined various ways by persons and organizations. We are not attempting a meticulous definition of this segment rather to know their composition broadly. According to Misra, the middle class population includes lecturers, writers, journalists, academicians, doctors, politicians, lawyers, engineers, architects, chemists, musicians, executives, businessmen, media personnel, philosophers, scientists, finance managers and others.[3] Pavan asserted, "… anybody who has a home to live in and can afford three meals a day, and has access to basic health care, public transport and schooling, with some disposable income to buy such basics as a fan or watch or cycle, has already climbed on to the middle class bandwagon."[4] Amalraj stated, "the emerging middle class people are literate, have access to all the technology, economic prosperity and play an important role in forming the public opinion in the nation."[5] According to McKinsey report of 2007, the household monthly income between ₹16,668 to ₹41,667 are seekers, ₹41,668 to ₹83,334 are strivers and are called middle class Indians.[6] Chatterjee stated that middle class income ranges from ₹20,001 to ₹86,000.[7] Lewis includes income, occupation, accent, spending habits, residence, culture, leisure pursuits, clothes education, moral attitudes and relationships with other individuals.[8] Aghamkar stated that middle class include middle range officers, clerks, teachers, nurses and college students.[9]

The Middle Class Indians: Origin and Development

The advent of the British in India brought a radical change in the status of social, political and economic patterns. In order to create a class equal to them, the British educational policy gave way for the Indians so that they would assist the administration and development of its internal resources in the country.[10] It was a small band of middle class Indians during 1900 under British rule but now India is soaring in terms of economy after the independence. Varma states, "For every seat in a technology institute there are thousands of aspirants."[11] McKinsey report reveals, one of the most striking findings is the recent growth that reduced the numbers of the poorest Indians, a group called deprived who earned less than 90,000 Indian rupees a year.[12] Misra says that the middle class social order did not grow from within the nation but rather, was implanted in India by the British without a commendable development in its economy and social institution.[13] The five-year plans that were introduced by Pt. Jawaharlal Nehru starting from 1951 and a reformation in 1991 during the time of Prime Minister P.V. Narasimha Rao changed the Indian economy dramatically. Rao resolved to bring the Indian economy into the 21st century by reducing the federal deficit and cutting inflation which attracted foreign investment and ultimately placed the opportunity for the growth of middle class segment.[14] Hence, India moved robustly from poverty to prosperity.

Importance of the Research

This project is important not only because of middle class being the fastest-growing segment and are influential but because the Gospel is for all. As stated earlier, in India the Gospel has had a great impact among the poor, rural and marginalized people which is well and good. Nevertheless, it is a vital need of the hour that the Gospel must penetrate to the middle class. This people group influences the society considerably through their dominance in journalism, the law, the bureaucracy, and others. They need the message of the love of Jesus Christ personally. Unfortunately, there is an assumption in the mind of the people that Gospel is for the poor or that Christianity is a poor religion. Here lies the importance to make known to the people that Gospel is for all. Rajendran stated, "The middle class and the rich need the Lord Jesus as much as anyone else."[15] Therefore, the contemporary Christians are called to reach the shakers and movers of the society as well with the Gospel.

Beneficiaries

This survey research would benefit the churches and mission agencies and any other mission practitioners who want to share the gospel to the influencers of this nation. This work would also help missionaries to understand the concept that middle class people have about God, sin, salvation, religion, prayers, view of their personal life, family life and others so as to share the Good News effectively to them.

Research Scope

This research was confined to seven major cities of India: Kolkata, Chennai, Bangalore, Pune, Ahmedabad, Nagpur and Guwahati. These cities were chosen as a sample to represent the cities of India as far as this research project is concern. The reason for choosing them was because they are the leading cities of India in terms of education, economy, population, IT and other areas of life.

Research Purpose

The main purpose of this survey was to find out how the middle class Indians could be served better with the love of Jesus Christ and document some of the models to serve this segment. Eventually, motivate the churches and missions to intentionally focus on the Indian middle class of other faiths so that they may be transformed by the message of the Gospel and in turn witness Christ to others.

Empirical Research Initiatives

Incepted in 1852, Interserve India, engaged in various ways in equipping and envisioning churches and missions. Out of several other new initiatives, Interserve has strongly felt the need of reaching middle class Indians of other faiths with the

Gospel message. Some of the organization's partners have started working among this segment and would like to encourage individuals, churches and mission agencies within India and abroad to serve this segment with the love of God.

Phase I

Phase I of the pilot survey on 'Serving Middle Class Indians' was conducted by the research team of Interserve India in five major cities of India viz.; Mumbai, Delhi, Hyderabad, Pune and Guwahati in 2009. In each city, 100 questionnaires were administered to people of both other faiths and Christians. Though the main target group was people of other faiths, feedback was also collected from Christians in order to have both views. The data were documented so that believers would be encouraged in reaching this segment individually and corporately. The respondents included people from Government services, doctors, engineers, lawyers, teachers, educationists, scholars, businessmen, professionals, house-wives and students. A brief summary findings of the phase I survey was published in Grassroots Mission Publications.[16]

Phase II

Phase II of the survey was aimed to extend the phase I study including other major cities located in different parts of India. The project started from the middle of 2010 and was completed by the end of 2011. In each city 1000 questionnaires were administered to middle class people from other faiths. In order to minimize some of the methodological errors, a standardized, validated questionnaire was used, employing a uniform methodology at all the selected cities in the survey. The analysis of the data as a whole and city-wise data was done in the National office at Pune by the research team under the supervision of the National Director of Interserve India.

Research Objectives

- To obtain a sample of demographic data to identify and understand middle class Indians better.

- To ascertain the actual context of the faith professed by the middle class Indians in terms of cognitive, affective and behavioural dimensions to determine spiritual change.

- To evolve strategies to reach out to the target audience in a relevant format in order that the churches and mission practitioners would be encouraged in reaching this segment.

- To initiate placement of more Interserve Partners and On Trackers and also encourage other mission practitioners in reaching out to this segment of people.

Expected Outcome

Churches and mission agencies would be informed about the importance of serving these people. In the Bible, Zaccheaus is a typical example of a middle-class urbanite exploiting and making money. An encounter with Jesus Christ transformed his life and he gave more than half of his wealth to the poor. This is the transformation we hope to see in the lives of the Indian middle class which in turn can transform the whole nation.

Method of the Field Research

Field research methodology included data collection in seven major cities of India through survey questionnaires from 1000 people of other faiths in each city. The essential components of the study design were; Cognitive, Affective and Behavioral. In order to collect 1000 feedbacks from people of other faiths,

15 to 25 Christian field-workers were engaged in each city and given 1300 to 1700 questionnaires depending on the demand. Over thousand feedback forms were collected in every city. We had to reject some which did not meet the required criteria and selected 1000 completed questionnaires. A proforma-questionnaire designed specifically for use in this project, was provided to the field-workers in each center only in English version. The field-workers contacted Christians who were working in various government offices, private and corporate offices, institutions and in the market places. And they in turn, gave the questionnaire to the people of other faiths in order to get feedback from them.

Sample Population

A total of 7000 individuals from other faiths were surveyed across seven major cities of India.

Study Questionnaires

Several meetings and discussions were held in the organization's office before and after designing the questionnaire with research experts and staff of Interserve India. The questionnaire was designed so as to learn the respondents' knowledge, attitudes, and practices. It was also prepared with options where the respondents would check only one closest to their opinion. The first section had 9 questions and was related to personal information such as gender, age distribution, education, marital status, sub-caste/people group, occupation, monthly household income, economic status, and religion.

The second section had 30 questions out of which 29 questions had options. The respondents had to mark one closest to their opinion. Each question also had an option of specify if any other. These options had space where the respondents would be able to write their opinion if s/he had any other opinion than the options given. The last question was open-ended, and the respondents had the freedom to express their thoughts.

The respondents were people of other faiths Indians who were into; Government service/Defence, Business, corporate service, Health care, Teaching/education, Information Technology/Engineering, Consultant/Professional, social work/ politics, media and others. Both male and female from different religions as such Hindu, Islam, Buddhists, Jain, Sikh, Atheist and ethnic religion were included.

Training of Fieldworkers

The field-workers were given a brief training so that they would understand the salient aspects of the research objectives, the structure of the questionnaires, and more importantly to be able to get feedback only from people of other faiths background in the context of middle-class Indians. They were also asked to strictly maintain the standard.

Questionnaire Administration

The Government offices, private company offices, schools, colleges, universities, tea stall, shops, train stations, airports, shopping malls, hospitals, India Institute of Management, India Institute of technology, house visits and marketplaces were randomly selected to get responses. The research coordinator of Interserve India office and field-workers carried out the task with the help of volunteers until the requisite sample (1000 feedbacks) was covered.

Project Monitoring

A standard protocol was developed for monitoring activities. This included; (a) submit the required budget (b) print the required number of questionnaires (c) contact people through phone calls (d) send Questionnaires through emails to the prospective field workers/volunteers (e) study the locations (f) book guest room for stay, etc.

Data Collection

In each selected city, the data were collected as hard copies filled by the respondents. Field workers were responsible to collect the printed questionnaires from the respondent as and when it was ready. The field-workers were provided data entry software and trained to use this software. Then, the data was entered to a computer database.

Research Findings: Socio-religious Perception of Middle-Class Indians of Other Faiths on their Knowledge, Attitude and Practice

A survey of the socio-religious perception of the contemporary middle class of other faiths people were studied in three levels (know, feel and action) in the light of selected major cities of India. However, the attempt to adhere to these three levels could not be achieved as desired. Nevertheless, the study focused on these aspects as much as possible. The perception of the sample population in the study was analysed. The vast economical, racial, religious, socio-political differences largely affect the way how to approach them in reaching the gospel to their context. Here goes the analysis.

Sample Demographics

The first section (Questions 1 – 9) of the survey primarily gives demographic information of the participants concerning their gender, age group, educational level, marital status, caste/ people group, occupation, household income, economic status, and their religion. The respondents were from various people groups with different religions.

Gender Division

The figure below shows the proportion of men and women in the study. We have collected views from both so that we have a balanced viewpoint. Out of 7000 respondents 54% were men and 45%, which means almost half of the respondents were women. 1% of the respondent preferred not to disclose their gender.

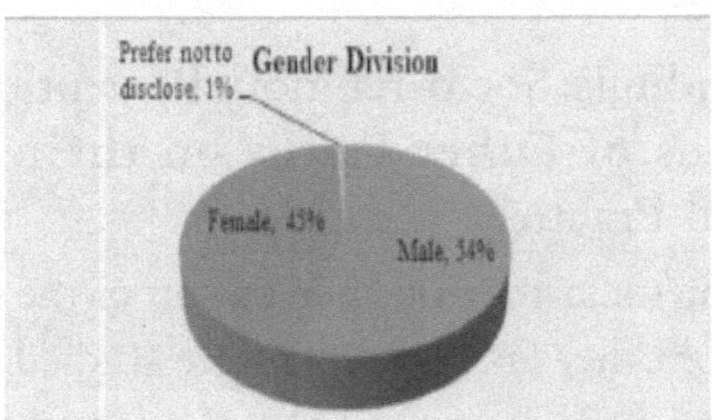

Age

45% of the respondents were below 25 years and 38% were between 26 – 40 years. 16% were between 41 – 60 years and another 1% was more than 61 years. This shows that an overwhelming 83% were below 40 years which means the respondents were quite young. Only 18% of the respondents were 41 years and above.

It is noteworthy that the survey reveals that young people were more open to share their opinion. In all the seven cities the respondents were very young and energetic. Reaching young Indian middle class with the Gospel would be strategic as they are open to share their opinion. They think positively and are open to change. The young generations are looking for new ideas and some are even willing to change to the new ideas. Moreover, most of them were bread-winners and are influencing the entire families, relatives and even their community.

Education Division

The below chart indicates that 40% of the respondents were graduates and 21% were post graduate. 26% of the respondents were college students and 11% of them studied till high school and 2% of them have no education. The respondents who claimed themselves as high school student and no education were into business. They had stopped their academic education and were engaged in successful business.

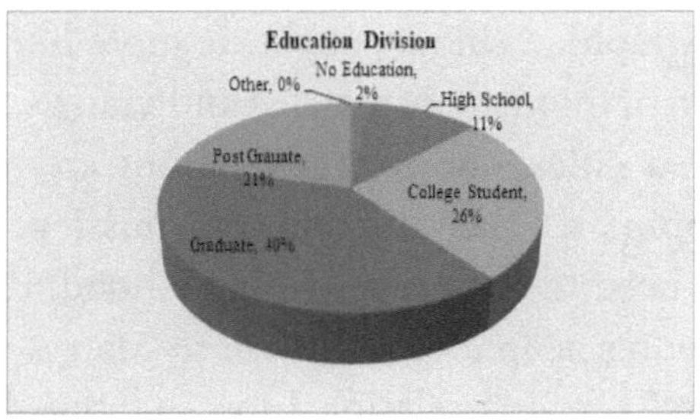

An overwhelming 87% of the respondents were educated people from college level to doctorate degree. This shows that highly educated people of India are open to share their opinion. Therefore, it is imperative to train educated Christians to witness the Gospel in order that educated people could be reached more effectively.

Marital Status

Here, 59% which is more than half of the study population were single. It is note-worthy that India is a young country. 36% of the study populations were married people. 3% of the respondents were divorced. Though the per cent is insignificant compared to the rest of the respondents, it is obvious that divorce is fast becoming a common practice in India.

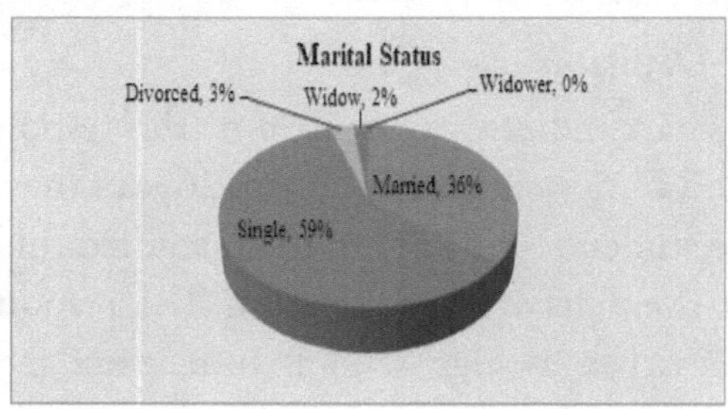

The survey shows that young people are more open to share their opinion in whichever way they think. Compared with overall demographics, single people are more likely to be open to share their opinion than married individuals. As is true to all the selected cities, younger generations are more open to share their opinion. The churches and missions need to pay considerable heed to the growing Single-hood, the increase in the age of young people who choose to marry, young people who practice "Live-in" relationships and the divorcees and widowers. The social stigma related to marital status does not affect the urban middle class as much among other classes.

Therefore, it would be imperative to focus more on these energetic influential people of our country.

Occupation Division

Concerning their occupation, respondents were from various backgrounds. Since we wanted to get from different opinions from diverse people, the sample selection was intentional. 25% of the respondents were teaching/education background. 19% of them were into government service and military personal. 13% of them were from corporate services. 11% were from IT/Engineering and another 11% were from health care. 10% were from business background. These people influenced the society at large. 4% of them were consultant and professionals in various fields. 2% were from social work and politics, while 2% were from media backgrounds. They were the bread-winners of the family.

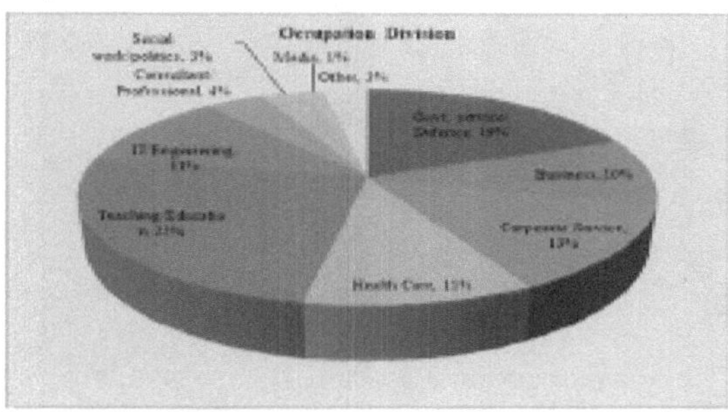

Interestingly, the survey proves that people who are still single and recently married are working in public and private sector largely. Though they are quite young they have the freedom to make decision. Moreover, they are quite responsive to new ideas if and when it is presented in their language. Peer pressure would be a stimulating force to reach these young people. In fact, younger generations are keener to learn new things in life. In reaching young Indian middle class, local church leaders should train younger generation to witness the gospel in their work places. Awareness campaign should be conducted in the local churches. Genuine Christian parents should encourage their sons and daughters to live out their life in words and deed in colleges, universities, Government offices, Private companies and in the business world.

Household Monthly Income

A good proportion, 41% stated that their income ranges from ₹16,668 to ₹41,667 and were termed as middle class. Another 40% of the respondents' income was between ₹7,500 to ₹16,667. This group also comes into the group of middle class and 14% stated that their income was between ₹41,667 to ₹83,334 and were yet to come in the category of middle class. Finally, 5% of them stated that their monthly household income was above ₹83,334. These categories of people were called as rich people.

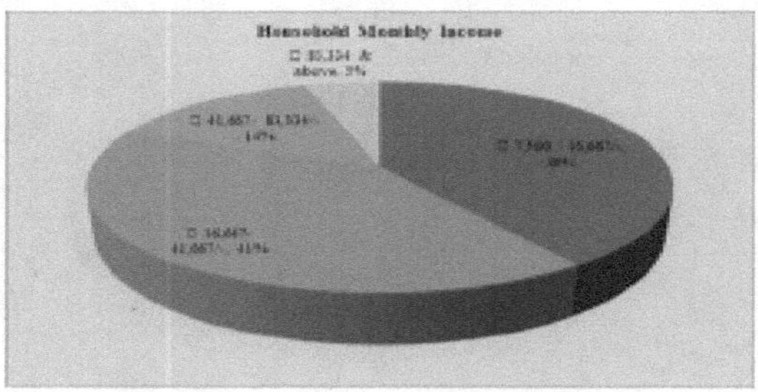

The survey shows that Indians are no more living in economically poor situation. It may be because of the people we chose to interview. 55% of the respondents we called Indian middle class as per our classification in this survey (education, values, cultural affinities, lifestyles, educational attainments and service sector employment.) The mission approach cannot be the same as it was before AD 2000. The vital need of the hour is reaching the middle class of the society without ignoring the poor people of the country. Creativity in planning to attract this segment is vital. Small group discussion would help in building relationship with these people and exchange of ideas and views may help creative planning to suit the target people.

Economic Status

Though we have our own classification, we are eager to learn from the respondents how they view their economic status. An overwhelming 87% said that they were from middle class. The other 8% stated that they are upper class. Therefore, we are confident to say that we hit our target audience in this survey. 5% of the study population stated that they are below poverty line. It is interesting to note that though some of the respondents are educated and earn a good salary working in a good offices, they still claim that they are below poverty line while some may not earn much still they claimed themselves as upper class.

The middle class is not only growing in terms of population but also influencing the nation in several ways like in politics, economics, social and others. Thus, reaching this segment which is the fastest growing segment is immediate need as far as the gospel is concern.

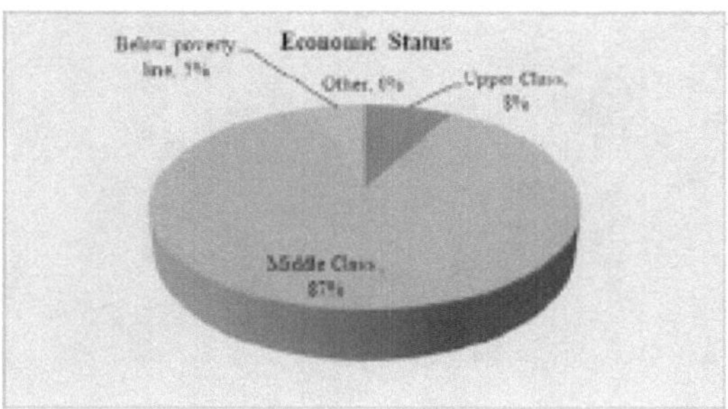

Religion

Without knowing what would be the response, we asked the respondents to tell us their religion. 74% of the respondents responded to our query saying that they are Hindus. Since Hinduism is the largest religion of India, majority of the respondents were from that religion. 12% of the respondents were from Islam background. 7% of them were Buddhist, 3% are from Jain. 2% claimed themselves as Sikh and 1% from ethnic religion. 1% of them claimed that they do not believe in any religion and some of them directly claimed that they are Atheist.

It is imperative to note that though there were people who were very upset when asked about their religion thinking that Christians were trying to convert them by doing these things. However, some were very cooperative. In one of the cities, we spoke to one young Muslim, who was a university student, about Christianity and Islam. He pointed out that Jesus is clearly mentioned in Koran. He was very interested to know about the uniqueness of Jesus Christ, and we explained to him.

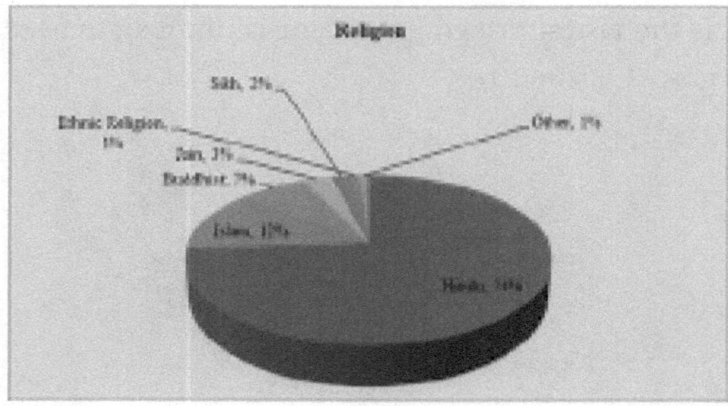

Perception of God

Introduction

Concept of God varies one from the other. Hinduism is commonly perceived as a polytheistic religion and belief in the philosophy of Pantheism. Pantheism considers everything, living and non-living, to be Divine and Sacred.[17] Muslims believe that everything belongs to God. "God is the Creator of everything.

He is the guardian over everything. Unto Him belong the keys of the heavens and the earth."[18] The difference is Hinduism says everything is God and Islam says everything is God's. Jainism does believe in God, not as a creator, but as a perfect being. They believe that living being is God.[19] Buddhism does not reject the belief in one God or many gods but accepted that the condition of a God is that of a being who through moral development is reborn in a happy state.[20] Sikhism teaches strict monotheism. There is only One God. But he can be conceived both as unattributed and attributed.[21] There are people who do not believe in the existence of God. An atheist is one who denies the existence of a deity or of divine beings. An agnostic is one who believes it impossible to know anything about God or about the creation of the universe and refrains from commitment to any religious doctrine. Infidel means an unbeliever, especially a nonbeliever in Islam or Christianity. A sceptic doubts and is critical of all accepted doctrines and creeds.[22]

Knowing God

Concerning the knowledge of God, the respondents' viewpoints were divided. 31% of the informants asserted that God is power. Some section of the other faiths worship God out of fear because they know God is powerful, dishonouring him will endanger their life. Another 31% believed that God is real. This shows that they believed the reality of God. 23% of the sample population stated that God is creator. This group thinking is very close to what Christians claimed. 5% of them said that God is unknowable. This idea is close to agnostics who believe that knowing God and his creation of the universe is impossible. Therefore, agnostic refrains from commitment to any religious doctrine. Though the percentage is insignificant, 4% of the sample populations directly claim that there is no God. They asserted that God is an illusion and God is unknowable. If we put together all these alike groups, then it is 13% which shows that among middle class segment there were quite a number of people who did not believe or were not sure about God. These people can be put together as Atheists, Agnostics, Infidels and skeptics as they don't believe in any gods or goddess.

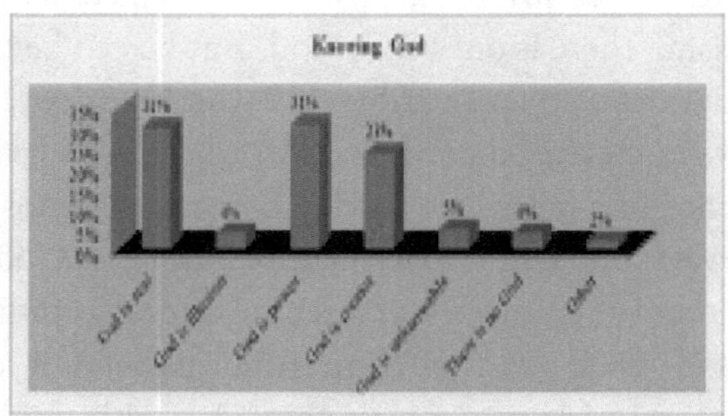

An overwhelming 85% of the study population believed that God is real, powerful and the creator. The Gospel may be shared with the middle class segment starting with God's creation of the universe and man and woman in His own image with the purpose of having intimate fellowship with him. Majority of the middle class believe in God. It is obvious that talking about Jesus is not an issue but introducing Jesus as the only God was the big challenge. As a Christian how do we share the uniqueness of Christ is important. Interestingly, among middle class population there are people who have no religious affiliation at all. However, majority of them were related to one religion or the other.

Attitude towards God

Any kind of feeling that arises in the mind is the result of consciousness, passion and inertia. Here, we asked the respondents about their feeling towards God. It is interesting to note that 44% of the respondents stated that they feel God's presence in their life. This helps us to know that middle class people are spiritual. 21% of them asserted that they love God and God loves them. This means they claim to have a close relationship with God, whichever God they believe in. 14% of them thought that God is for people who need him. They might have thought that only in times of troubles or sometimes in certain occasion people need otherwise it is not necessary. 12% of them stated that they experience God's love. This could be merged with option one and three. 9% of the respondents asserted that they feel nothing about God in their life.

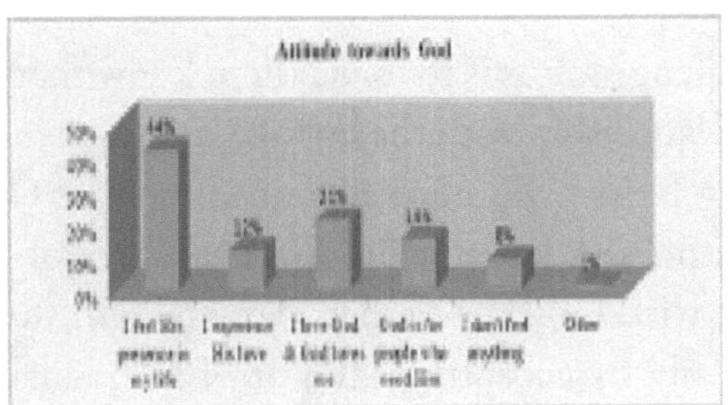

The survey shows that 77% of the study population have close contact with whichever God they worshipped. It is a fact that the middle class people feel God's presence in their life. The challenge is to make them know that Christ is the only way to eternal life. There are many opportunities that can be created to reach out to these 'God-fearers' and build bridges to communicate the love of Christ effectively.

Relationship with God

It is stimulating to learn that 44% of the respondents believed that doing good things to living beings is an act of worshipping God. 23% of the informants indicated that they communicate with God. We are not clear in what way they communicate to God, but it is interesting that they believe in communicating with their God. 21% of them said that they obey their Scriptures or Holy Book. 11% of them say that they do not know whether they are relating in any way to their God.

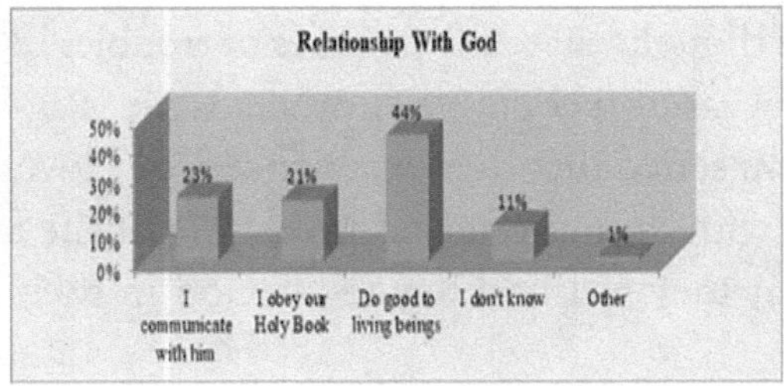

The challenge for us is to make them know that we can have a personal relationship with the loving God just as a child relates to his loving father. We need to introduce that God loved us and gave us his son Jesus to die for us and restore the broken relationship with God the Father. Now relationship with God is possible only by accepting the gift of reconciliation offered through His Son Jesus.

Conclusion

We asked the respondents about their knowledge, attitude and action about God. The feedback we received from them was interesting. This survey concludes that majority of the middle class Indians believed in God and understood God as powerful, and feel his presence in their life and doing good things to other human beings is act of worshipping and relating to God.

Therefore, in attempting to reach the middle class with gospel we may not need to talk about God, but emphasis must be on the redemptive work of God through Jesus Christ.

Perception of Sin

Introduction

In this section, we are trying to learn the concept of sin by the other faiths. We may say sin is missing the mark but what would people of other faiths say about it. It would be interesting to learn the concept of other faiths to serve them better with the Good News.

Meaning of Sin

When asked about the meaning of sin, the respondents understood differently. 33% of the informants stated that sin means violating moral and ethical codes. Ethical may mean a system of moral principles concerning appropriate conduct for an individual or group violating a moral standard and how they affect behaviour. 28% of them said sin means ignorance of truth. It means people commit sin because they do not know the truth. Another 27% suggested that sin means breaking God's law. This view is somewhat close to the understanding of Christians. 10% suggested that murder, adultery, and any other kind of unpleasant act are sin.

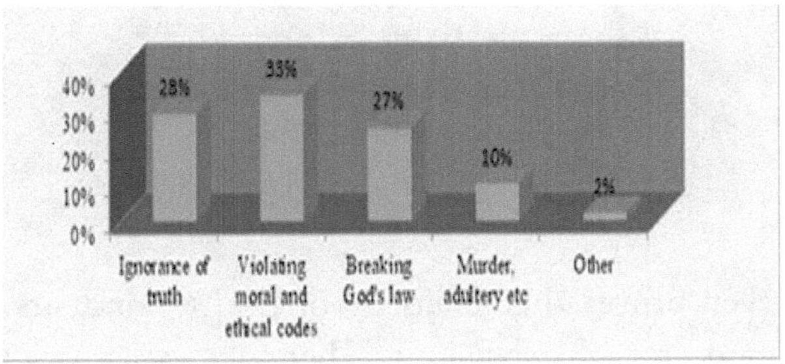

We learnt through interaction and through questionnaire that people of other faiths were aware about sin. We need to address this concern to make them know that all human beings need Jesus Christ who has the authority to forgive sin.

Who is Sinner?

Concerning sin, we asked if everyone is a sinner. 46% of the respondents suggested that everyone commits sin. This opinion is close to the belief of Christians. This will be a good place to start sharing the gospel to the other faiths in the light of the scripture where it says everyone is a sinner. 24% of them suggested that only some people commit sin. 8% of them stated there are some people who never commit sin. Option (b) and (c) has the same meaning. The idea is that there are people who are sinless. This is against the teaching of Bible. 21% of them did not know about sin. The research team was surprised to learn that there are many people who do not know about sin and its meaning. One of the most asked questions from the respondents while filling the questionnaire was about sin.

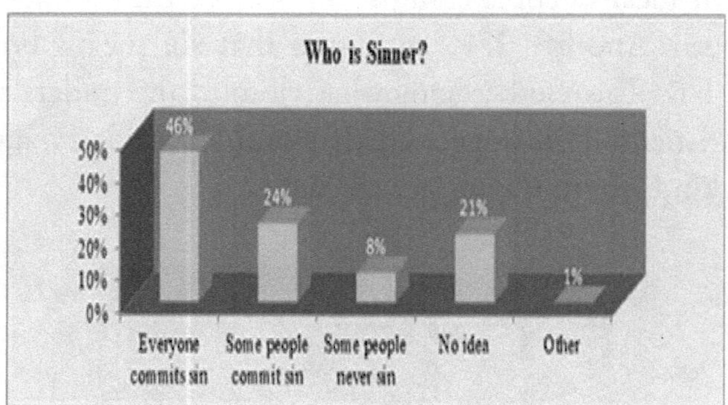

The survey proves that majority of the respondents do not understand properly what sin is. Therefore, explaining to them the origin of sin and the solution provided by God is one of the conversation starters among the middle class.

Forgiveness of Sin

Without knowing what would be their response, we asked the means and ways of forgiveness to those who commit sin. An overwhelming 67% suggested that one can be forgiven through their good works. 11% of them honestly stated that they don't know how the sinner can be forgiven. These people were honest in saying they do not know. 9% of them suggested that someone can be forgiven from their sin through the blood of Jesus Christ. These people must have heard about Jesus and his redemptive work though they are not into the family. Another 8% suggested that there is no way for the forgiveness of sin.

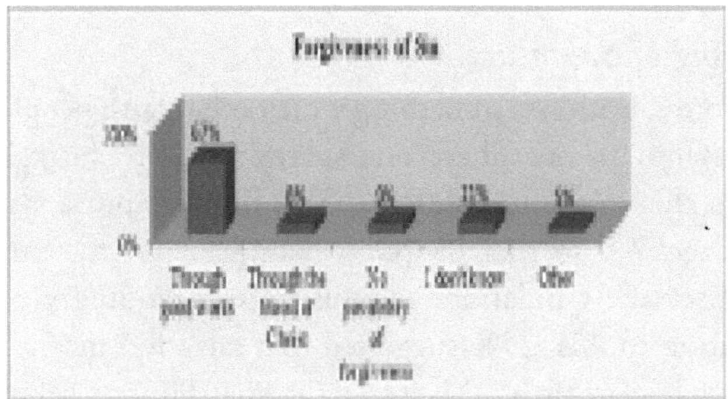

Since majority of the study population thought that forgiveness of sin can be found through good work, we need to make them know that good work without Christ has no meaning as far as salvation is concerned.

Conclusion

People of other faiths understood sin differently. There were people who were not convinced that they were sinners.

As mission practitioners, we are called to be prepared to answer the need when presenting the gospel to the other faiths.

Perception of Salvation

Introduction

As a Christian, our understanding of salvation would be the redemption of human from the bondage of sin and liability to eternal death, and the conferring on him of everlasting happiness. "… God's gift of salvation is available only through the atoning death of the historical person, Jesus of Nazareth, and is appropriated through explicit faith in Jesus…"[23] On the other hand, understanding of people of other faiths may be different from what we claim. Let us see how the survey shows on this matter.

Meaning of Salvation

The word salvation is something which other faith people never understand. In our phase one survey we were struggling to explain this to the respondents. This time we put a synonym word '*moksha*' so that people will understand the meaning. As we see the tabulation, there is no outstanding viewpoint in relation to this. 29% suggested that salvation means release from cycle of rebirth. This is exactly what Hindus belief. 28% of them stated that they don't know about salvation. Another 27% of the respondents asserted that salvation means eternal life. This is exactly what Hindus believe. 27% of the respondents believe salvation means eternal life. This is close to Christian belief concerning salvation. They may be receptive to the gospel if they understand the redemptive work of Christ. Another 15% stated that salvation means saving from eternal grief. This option can be merged with option (a) which says eternal life. Then, we can say 42% of them understand salvation as connected to eternal life.

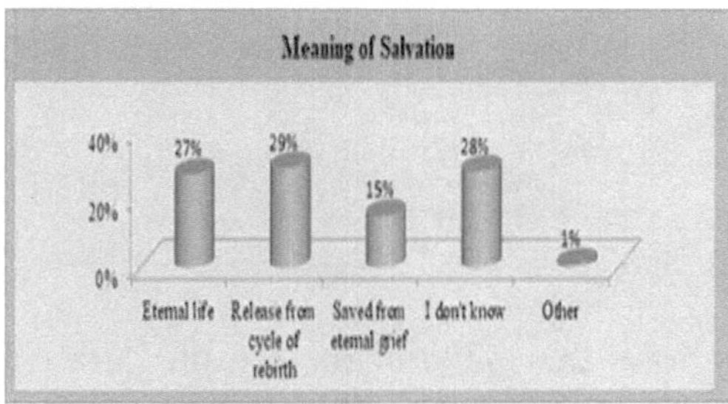

The survey concludes that while there are people who are conscious about their eternal life some are not sure about it. We need to help people to reflect on life after death and then share the hope of resurrection and eternal life through which we can communicate the Good News.

Christian Concept of Salvation

In connection with the Christian claim of "Jesus is the only way to salvation" 44% of the respondents chose the option 'I disagree'. People of other faiths strongly believe that Jesus was one of the ways to salvation among many other gods and goddesses. Surprisingly, 30% of the respondents suggested that they agreed with this statement while many others were very upset with this claim. We asked one of the respondents with whom we became friendly after a short discussion why he agreed with this claim. The answer was: "for Christians Jesus is the way to salvation, for Muslims, Allah, and so on." The bottom line is one god with different names. 22% of the respondents stated they don't care whether Jesus is the only way to salvation or not.

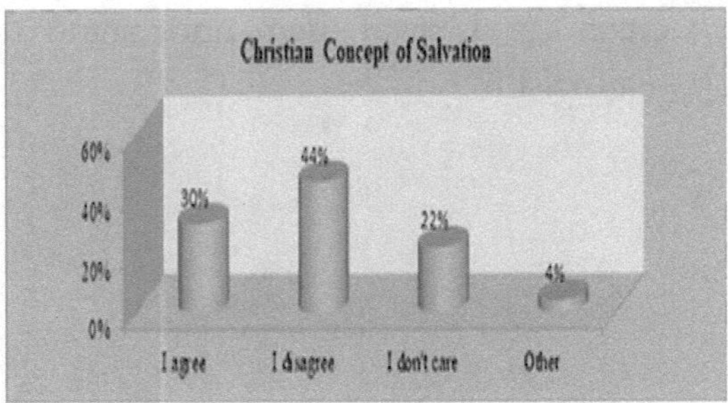

The survey shows that 57% of the sample data is found to be mild concerning the claim Jesus is the only way to salvation. We wrongly assume that people of other faiths are strongly against Christians. It is proved that majority of the population are either undecided or are interested in the claims of Jesus Christ.

Attaining Salvation

We asked, what should you do to attain salvation? 41%, which is the highest percentage asserted that in order to attain salvation one must do good deeds. 38% of them said that having faith in God and 38% stated that perfection in daily living.

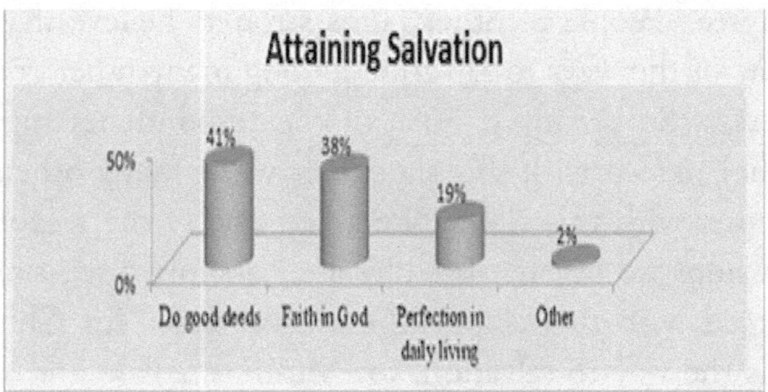

The survey indicates that majority of other faiths believe in doing good works so as to attain salvation. Serving them through holistic ministry would be the key.

Conclusion

It is interesting to asked people of other faiths who have different notion concerning salvation. Though the term salvation is a Christian jargon we have added moksha so that people of other faiths could understand the meaning in a clearer way. Majority of the respondents think that salvation could be attain through doing good works.

Perception of Prayer

Introduction

We believe prayer is the integral part of our Christian life. It could be either individual or communal and take place in public or in private with many reasons such as personal or common well beings. All of us whether rich or poor, big or small, long to connect with someone who can identify with our circumstances in our joy or sadness.

What is Prayer?

We were interested to learn about the concept of prayer from different people. 43% of the study population stated that prayer is talking to God. This is somewhat close to Christian's concept on prayer. Since it is acceptable for many among other faiths, prayer would be one important way to share the love of Christ. 29% stated that prayer is essential in life. It is obvious that there were many people of other faiths who considered prayer very crucial. 24% of them stated that prayer was everyday ritual life. For only 3% prayer did not mean anything.

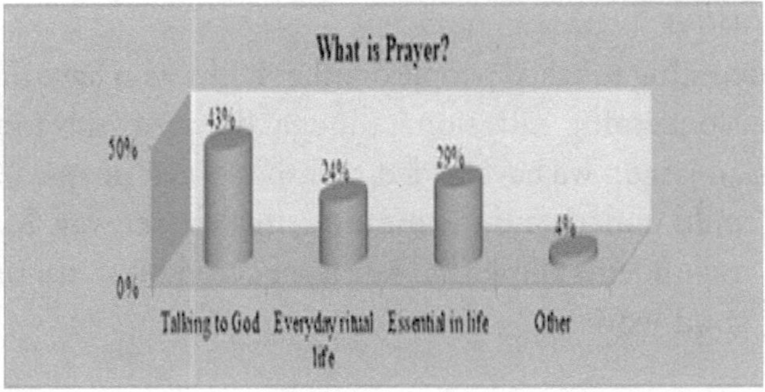

The survey shows that 72% of the study populations understand that prayer is talking to God and also essential in life. Our Bible encourages us to intercede for others. People of other faiths normally accept praying for them. Taking this advantage, we can invite them for meal or just a cup of coffee and pray for them so that they will come to know the love of Christ.

Does Prayer Work?

We were curious to know whether people of other faiths believed that prayer can change God's mind. It is interesting to learn the 43% of the respondents believed that honest prayer can change God's mind. Another 22% believed that it depends on the person. In other words, God would change his mind if only the person is good. We need to educate this group that we are righteous before God only through Jesus Christ. Surprisingly, 19% of them said they don't know whether God would change his mind through prayer. This people might not experience the power of prayer. Another 14% said that sometimes God changed his mind.

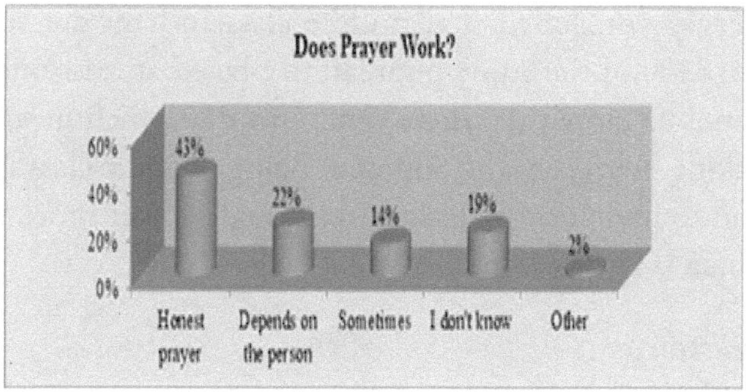

The middle class Indians who believe in the effect of prayer are the right people with whom we can start building bridges by praying with them and for them so that they can experience the power of God's intervention. We need to communicate that when we pray in faith, God is ready to answer our prayer.

Prayer Time

We intended to know about the prayer life of middle class. We asked how many times they pray to their God. The response did not show any outstanding percentage. 35% of them stated that they prayed one time in a day. 26% claimed that they prayed two times and another 20% stated that they prayed more than three times in a day. Surprisingly, 15% of them said that they did not pray.

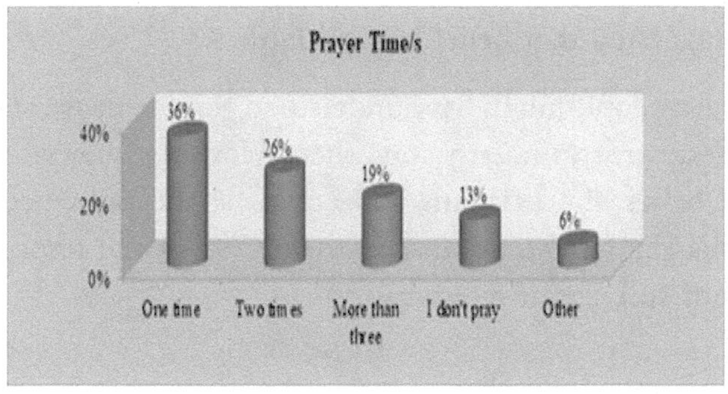

The survey concluded that middle class Indians are spiritual people. 81% of the study population prayed at least one time, two times or more than three times in a day which means they are seeking help from the Supreme Being. Middle class Indians respond to invitation to pray and through prayer times we can introduce them to Jesus Christ.

Conclusion

Though there are people who do not believe in prayer, the survey proved that majority of the study population believed in prayer. Prayer ministry would be one of the most effective ways of serving the middle class segment.

Perception of Religion

Introduction

In order to learn how people of other faiths understood religion, we decided to ask related question on their knowledge, attitude and practice about religion.

Understanding of Religion

Asked about their understanding of religion, 37% of them suggested that religion is human-made. 30% of them suggested that religion is our belief. Probably, these people think religion is simply a mental act, or a habit of placing trust in someone. 25% suggested that belief is good faith.

These people might have understood good faith as a standard of honesty, trust, sincerity and others. However, they were close to the belief of Christians and could be the right people to start sharing Christian faith to them. 7% of the respondents were not sure about religion.

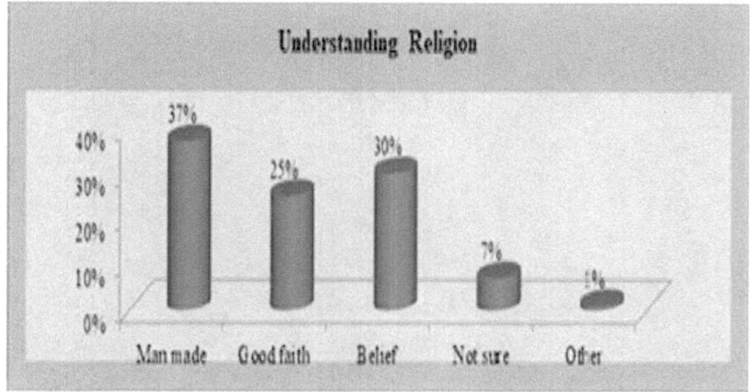

We are reminded that many Hindus believed that religion is human-made attempt to reach God. They also believed that God is everything and human itself is God because God is within. Concerning the concept of religion, the opinions are varied. The option (b) and (c) is adjacent with the concept of Christianity. Therefore, serving this people with the gospel would be the right start.

What Determines Religion of a Person?

In answering the question, what determines religion of a person? 48% which was the highest percentages in this table stated that it is by birth. In other words, if a person born in a Hindu family should be Hindu, to Muslim, Muslim etc. The next highest 33% goes to people who chose the option personal decision. These people must have thought that individual has the right to choose their religion as they wish. 17% of them suggested that family should decide the matter.

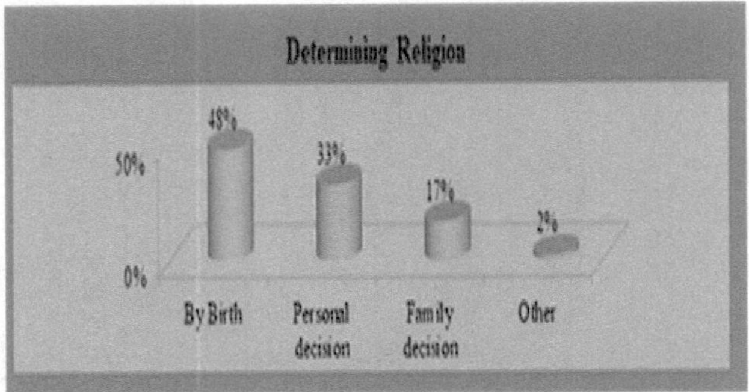

The survey shows that there are quite number of people who think independently when it comes to religion. They suggest that people should decide whichever religion they are comfortable. Here is an opportunity where we can take the gospel to the people who think independently on one hand and to others sharing the Good News to the whole family may be the right start.

Changing Religion

We decided to make a statement; one should not change his/her religion. It was interesting to see that 41% said they disagree. These people really mean to say that one has the right to choose their religion. 40% of the study population agreed with the statement. It is imperative to note that while we thought people of other faiths are very rigid in their belief, here are people who thought independently. Another 17% of the respondents said that they don't know. These people must be not interested in religion at all. 2% of them chose the option, if any other. Most of them suggested that we cannot interfere in somebody's life saying go for this or that religion.

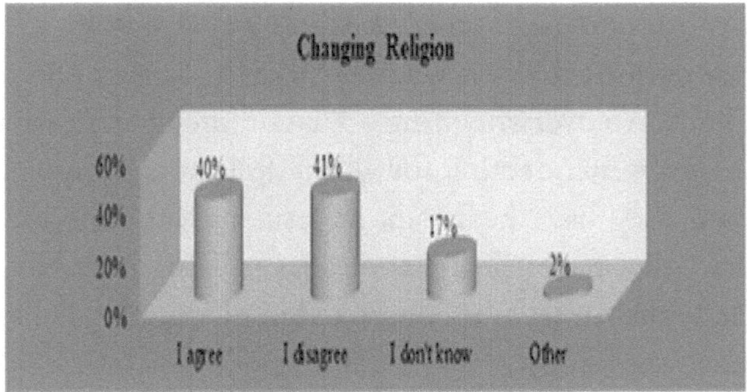

This survey concludes that there are certain people who are very open to any religion. In that sense, as mission practitioners if we contact people individually and share the gospel to them in their language, they would be more receptive.

Conclusion

The survey concluded that majority of the middle class people believed that religion is just human-made. This is by birth and people need not to change their religion. However, there is a significant proportion of people who are independent in their decision making and will be open to consider the claims of Jesus Christ if communicated contextually, without any confrontation.

Perception of Jesus Christ

Introduction

We intended to know how people think about Jesus Christ. In relation to that we prepared three questions which would help to identify how they know, feel and do in connection to the person, Jesus Christ.

Number of Time of Hearing about Jesus Christ

We were curious to learn whether people of other faiths heard about Jesus. An overwhelming 73% said they had heard several times. This is encouraging for all the followers of Jesus Christ. 18% said they have heard about Jesus at least one time. 9% said that they never heard about Jesus. This may have been possible as the survey was conducted in places where Christians were not well known.

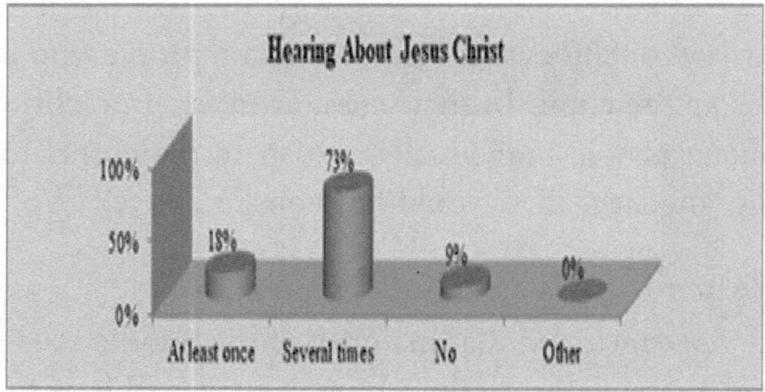

This survey shows that high proportion of other faiths had heard about Jesus Christ. This is encouraging, but how did they first hear about Jesus matters because that will have lasting impression. We need to focus more on his divinity, because people might have heard about his humanity.

Ways of Hearing about Jesus Christ

We intended to know how they heard about Jesus to reach them more effectively. It is interesting to learn that 36% which is the highest percentage shared that they have heard about Jesus through their friends. Here, we learn that sharing the Gospel through friends' circle would be effective. 26% of the respondents shared that through school they have heard about Jesus. Christians have always done a great work in the field of education. Another 17% said that through books they have come across the name Jesus. As we know middle class people are educated. They have read Christian books and many of them said they have read the scripture. 9% of them said they have heard Jesus through television. 5% and 4% of them said through internet and movies. We can conclude that media plays a great role in spreading the name of Jesus.

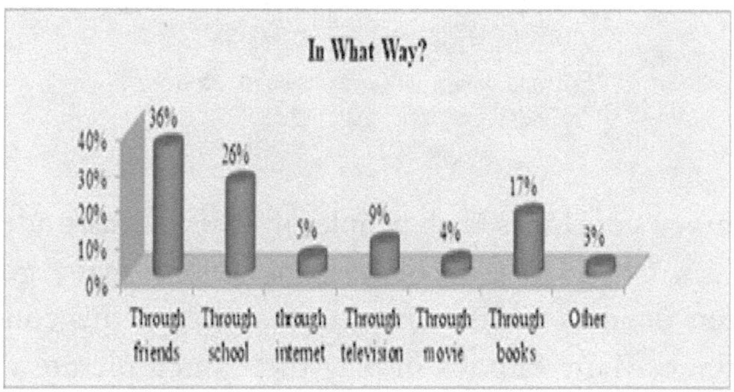

The survey shows that personal evangelism based on relationship building among friends and educational institutions would be the best means and ways of communicating Jesus among the other faiths of middle class.

Who is Jesus?

Concerning Jesus, we asked the respondents "who do you say Jesus is." The answers were scattered and therefore no significant percentage has emerged. 33% of them suggested that Jesus is Christian God. This shows that though they know who Jesus is, they do not know who he really is. 26% of them suggested that Jesus is one among the many gods. 24% of the respondents suggested that Jesus is a great teacher. These respondents may have read or heard about the teachings of Jesus in the book of Gospels. They did not know his divinity but know his humanity. 18% of the respondents amazingly stated that Jesus is saviour of humankind. These people would be strategic to start sharing the gospel.

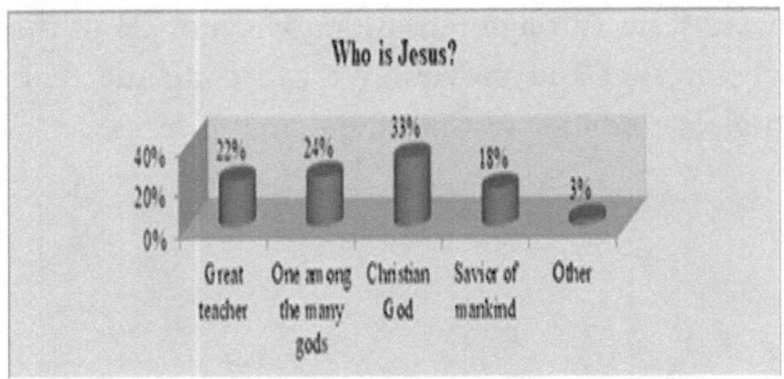

The survey concludes that people of other faiths understood Jesus as a Christian God or just one among many gods. As followers of Jesus Christ how do we addresses this concept is important. Many Hindus display the framed picture of Jesus among many other gods and goddesses in their homes and offices. This is a big challenge for us how to take the name Jesus as the only God. In this pluralistic context taking the gospel, particularly to the middle class people is a big challenge. They have no problem in agreeing to say Jesus is God but do not believe that he is the only God.

Conclusion

An overwhelming majority of the study population asserted that they have heard and know Jesus through their friends and eventually they think that he is a Christian God. Using this as a point of contact we need to communicate the Good News effectively so that many may hear and accept the truth.

Perception of Personal Life

Introduction

India is changing rapidly in all spheres of life. We wanted to know about the issues regarding the personal life of individuals to address the need of middle class with the love of God. Like others, here too we have three different questions concerning a person's life.

View of Life

We asked the respondents as to how they viewed their personal life. 37% of the respondents shared that they view their personal life as normal. 32% of them said that they have a peaceful life. 22% of them viewed as short and precious. 8% though it is less in percentage honestly spelt out their life as stressful.

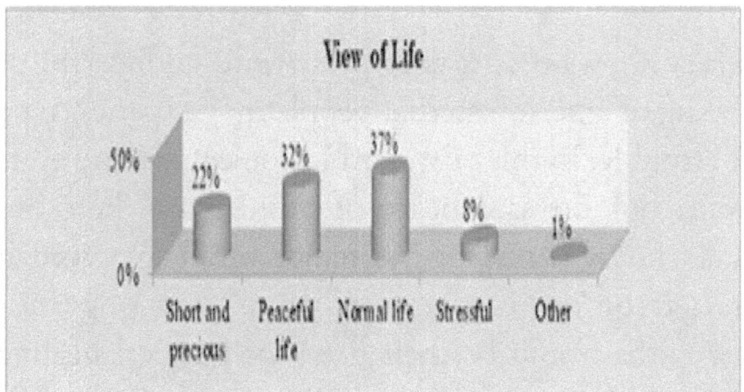

The survey records that there are people who are struggling with life and need help to overcome stress and also there are people who see their life as short and precious. We can serve this group of people by introducing Jesus Christ who can bring fulfillment to their lives.

Daily Need

It is interesting to learn that 47% of the respondents said the greatest need in their personal life was peace of mind. 32% of them said that they need good health the most. 11% said richness is what they need the most. And 9% of them suggested that security was a big concern for them.

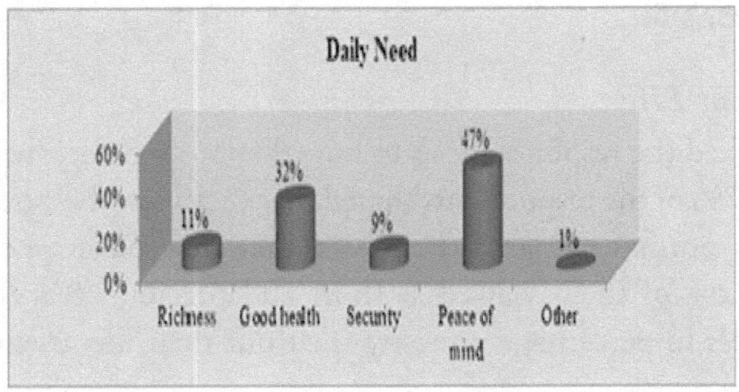

The survey shows that it is imperative to address the state of inner being of a person so that people may experience peace in times of trouble. In this busy world people may have everything they want but the said peace of mind is nowhere but with Christ. Sickness is one of the major problems faced by any human here on this earth and to minister among the people of other faiths would be their need for physical healing. In a world of violence, security is a big concern for a significant group of respondents.

Life Challenge

A high proportion 60% asserted that to address life challenges they need to work hard. 21% of them said that they summit to God. This practice is very close to Christians. 14% said that they shared their problems with their friends. 4% of them try to keep away from others.

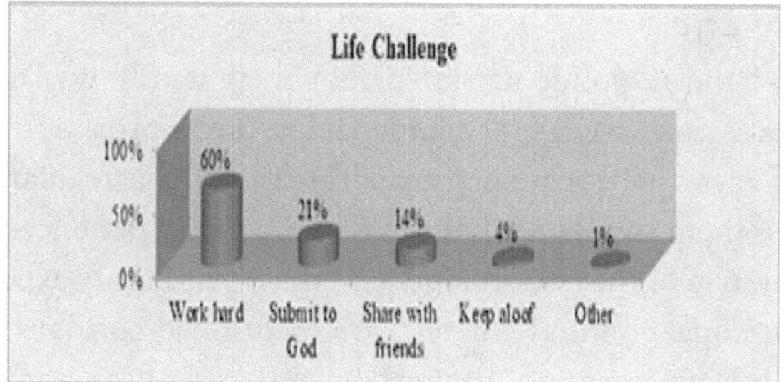

People find different means and ways when it comes to responding to life's challenges. It is true that middle class segment works very hard to achieve their aspirations and desires. At the same time, they value relationships and seek to socialize and build communities. During this, a few fall prey to loneliness. There are many opportunities to serve people with these inner-most need with the love of Christ.

Conclusion

We assume that people who are affluent like the middle class may not have many needs. However, the survey concludes that even though they may not have physical needs, they have many social and spiritual needs. It is the challenge for mission practioners to develop ministry models that will meet these needs and open the doors for the middle class to enter the Kingdom of God.

Perception of Family Life

Introduction

In this section we wanted to learn the concept of family by the middle class of other faiths. We have asked in three ways to get the clearer picture so that we will understand better and serve them effectively.

Family Life

46% of the respondents stated that their family was normal. Normal means average or standard. In other words, normal life would mean performing proper functions in a regular form. 43% of them suggested that their family had experienced peace and joy. 6% of the respondents said that their family experience interpersonal conflicts whereas 5% mentioned constant worry. From this we learn that though the majority of the population stated that their family is normal or that they had peaceful lives, some people experienced difficult situation. We need to address these issues.

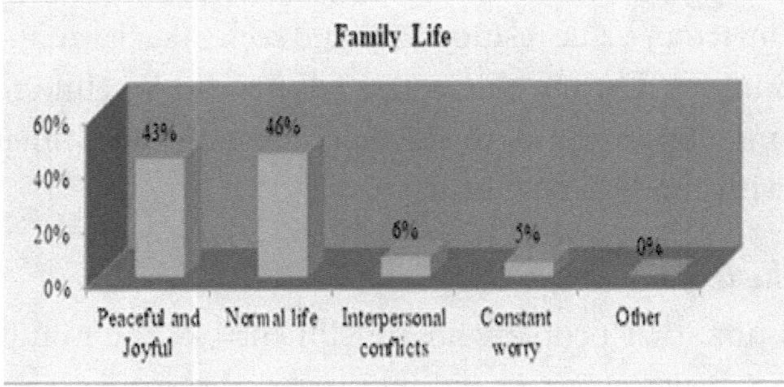

The survey proves that majority of Indian middle class families have normal and peaceful life. However, we need to consider that family honour is an important value among middle class and many will not disclose their difficulties to strangers. However, there are quite number of people who need special attention to overcome conflicts among family members which led to constant worries. As mission practitioners addressing this issue would be important for the furtherance of God's kingdom.

Family Daily Need

Not knowing what their choice would be, we asked about their family main need. 40% of them said happiness. This helps us to understand that people are looking for happiness in their family. Many families would claim that they have normal life in their family still happiness is missing. 19% of them felt health as the chief need. 18% of them declared finance as the major concern. 14% stated safety is the most need. 8% of them said children education.

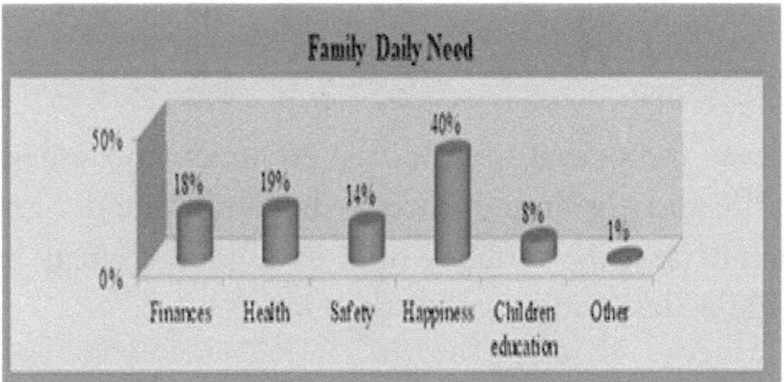

Here, it is obvious that a good percentage falls on happiness. Family needs are a priority among the middle classes. Significant percentage of respondents has stated that finance, health and children's education as their needs. Mission practioners need to develop models of ministry that will meet these needs among the families.

Family Struggle

Knowing how people handle struggle is another area we were interested in. We asked from the respondents concerning how they handled struggle. 65% of the respondents stated that they handle struggles through family discussion. We learn that among middle class section family bond is still very strong. 18% of them said that everyone has the right to think in their own way. Here we learn that among middle class there are people who think the way western people think. 16% of them said they consult experts and elders as and when family encounters a problem.

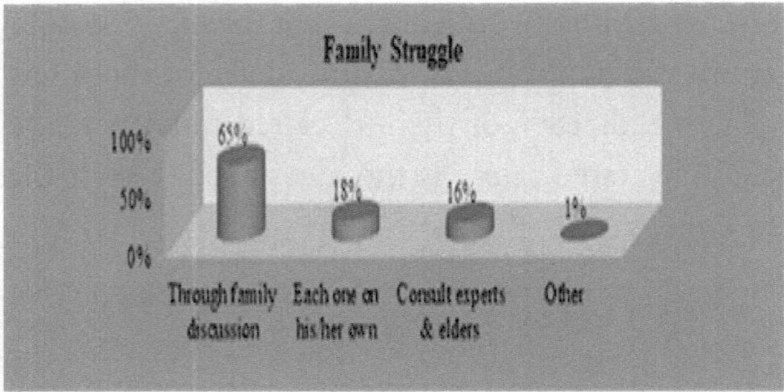

The survey shows that middle class are much concerned about family life and give importance to the family bond. Serving all the members of the family would be a good strategy to serve the middle class Indians with the Gospel.

Conclusion

In responding to family challenges, many people stated that they discuss issues in the family. But there are people who are looking for experts to help them solve their problems. We need Christian family counsellors and mentors who can serve young urban middle class families.

Perception of Christians

Introduction

This section seeks to find the attitude of people of other faiths towards Christians. One of the things which always is in our mind is how people of other faiths perceive the followers of Jesus Christ. Let us see how they respond in connection with this.

Knowing Christians

We asked what they know about Christians. To our surprise 29% which is the highest percentage said that they did not know. 27% of them said that Christians were educated people. 20% said that Christians were followers of western culture.

11% said that Christians were affluent people but 8% thought that Christians were poor people.

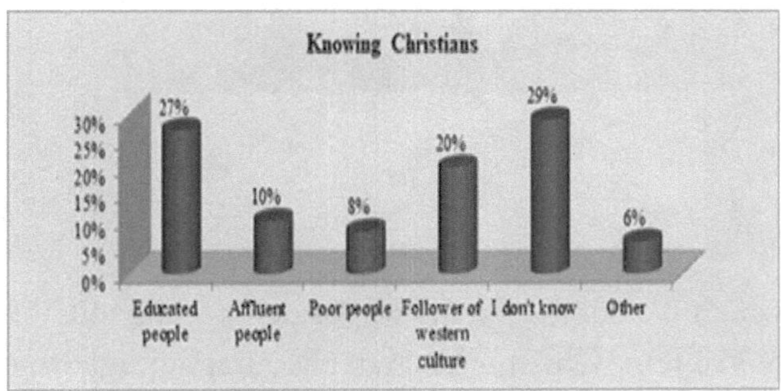

Since the highest percentage is not decided, we may conclude that people of other faiths observe Christians as educated people. There are significant percentages of people who still perceive Christians are followers of Western culture. This challenges us to reflect on how we portray Christ in our life, worship and practices. Initially, Christians were looked upon as poor people but now this attitude has changed significantly.

Attitude towards Christians

We intended to learn the feelings of people of other faiths to the follower of Jesus Christ 30% of them said they did not have any idea. 29% said Christians were people of good moral character. 26% respondents said that they are happy people. 11% said that Christians are self-centred people. They must have said this because Christians normally do not participate in their festivals. Any way, it's interesting that we are perceived in that way.

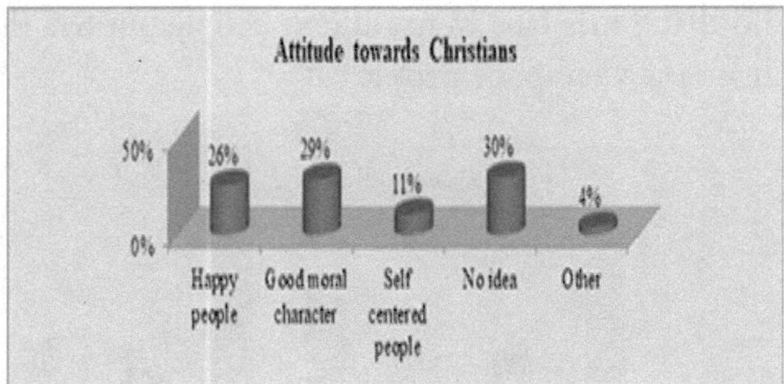

54% which is majority of the respondents feel good about the followers of Jesus Christ. This is an encouraging sign for us. The expectations that Christians have a higher standard of moral character give us more responsibility as we live out our faith. It is interesting that some perceive us as self-centred people which may refer to our practice of not participating in community events and occupied with our own religious observances and traditions. We are an open book and we must live out Christ through our lives.

Relationship with Christians

A high proportion of 60% stated that the followers of Jesus Christ were their good friend. Another 17% said that they did not have any relationship with Christians. Another 13% said that they had Christian neighbours, while 8% of them said they had Christian relatives.

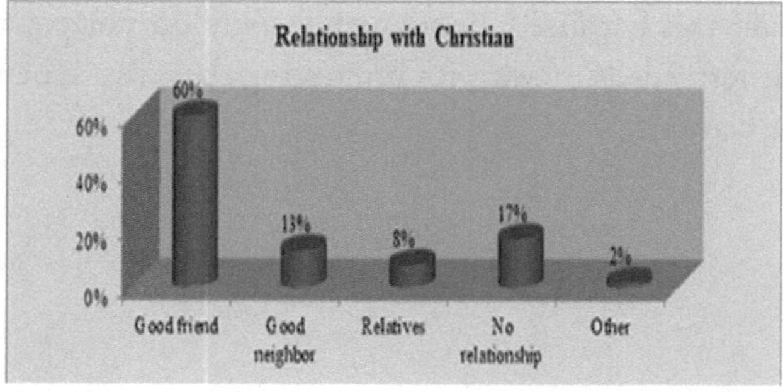

The survey shows that majority of the respondents know Christians through various ways, be it neighbour, relatives or friends. Relationship is always the beginning where we can start sharing the good news to other faiths. Christians have done a good job in terms of making friendships with the other faiths. Christians should be encouraged to have close connection with other faiths and share Christ through words and action. Here, the need would be encouraging Christians to witness Christ to their neighbours, friends and relatives.

Conclusion

The survey suggests that as far as possible middle class people of other faiths tried to avoid commenting on Christians. Many of them suggested that they (Christians) are like any other human beings. It is encouraging to note that high proportion of people of other faiths stated that Christians are their good friend. This is a healthy sign for Christian as a whole. Personal relationship is the basis to start communicating the Gospel to the people of other faiths.

Christians' Role in the Society

The respondents were asked, what they would say about Christian's role in the society. 40% of the respondents suggested that imparting education to the society. 30% of them said that Christians change their values. 21% said Christians are western culture follower.

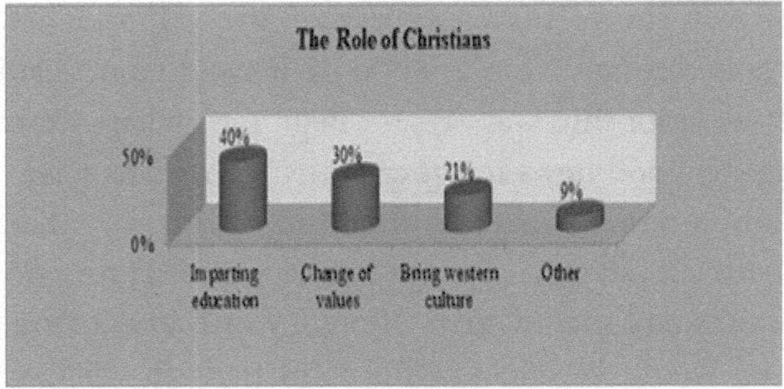

We see that the perception of other faiths toward Christians is changing. From this we could learn that people of other faiths observed that we have contributed to the society. Education is still relevant in reaching the Gospel to the other faiths. We need to be careful in our adaptation of the western practices even though fewer percentages of people view us in this manner. We need to find other avenues of involvement and contribution to the society and nation building.

Choosing Christianity

As stated earlier, though we tried to look at three levels we have just one question in connection with the reason why middle class of other faiths chose to become the follower of Jesus Christ.

We were very interested to learn from the people of other faiths about their opinion concerning the reason of the middle class of other faiths to become the follower of Jesus Christ. 26% of the respondents stated that because of good example of Jesus Christ. Another 24% of them suggested that because of children's education they choose to follow Jesus Christ. This may be true to certain extent because one of the major concerns of middle class people is the education of their children. Another 21% said because of social status.

The perception of the people of other faiths about those who choose to follow Jesus Christ shows that 68% of adopted Christianity for their personal benefit. It is interesting that this is a strong perception and we need to tell stories of transformation of those who follow Christ. However, 23% rightly stated that because of the exemplary life of Jesus Christ. There are a significant people who choose because of social status. This is a difficult issue and mission practioners must address this as more people from the most backward communities and Dalits attain middle class status and consider following Jesus Christ.

Conclusion

It is important to understand what others perceive about us as we attempt to communicate the Good News. We need to ensure that our communication is not misunderstood by the recipients. From these studies we learn how to be more effective in our service to the communities around us. All these data provide baseline information, evidence for prioritizing interventions and collecting in-depth knowledge about how to impact lives and communities. Conducting the middle class survey enriches and informs mission practitioners to serve communities wide with credible basis for strategic decision-making.

Summary and Recommendations

The nature of this study implies that relevant recommendations should be addressed to the churches and mission organizations for interventions. Also, individuals and mission practitioners interested in serving the middle class segment with the Gospel could use this.

The following recommendations are direct results of the empirical research of the study population among seven major cities of India.

1. Majority of middle class Indians are spiritually minded and believe in God. Their concept of God may be different, but we have a common ground on which to build relationships and start conversations.

2. The people of other faiths from middle class have a consciousness about sin but are not sure about the forgiveness of sin. Communicating the Good news of forgiveness of sin through Jesus Christ should form a major content of our message.

3. People of other faiths believe the Jesus is one of the ways to salvation. The challenge for us is to effectively communicate the uniqueness of Jesus Christ.

4. Majority of them give importance to prayer and believe in its effectiveness. Therefore, prayer ministry is a great tool to reach out to middle class people.

5. The opinion that Christianity is a foreign religion is diminishing. We need to continue to contextualize the practice of our faith to build bridges with various communities.

6. Even though a smaller percentage of people have indicated that changing religion is a personal choice, it is a growing trend. We should encourage families and individuals to consider the claims of Jesus Christ and make decisions to follow him.

7. The middle class people may not have physical or financial needs but seek peace of mind and safety in their personal and family life. We need to create opportunities to serve the needs among families.

8. People of other faiths appreciate the contributions of Christians in the field of education. We need to continue our educational ministry by strengthening the vision of the existing institutions and start many more educational institutions to cater to the huge need.

9. We need to tell the stories of transformation of individuals and communities so that the nation will know that those who decide to follow Christ have made a spiritual decision.

10. Women play a major role in public and private offices influencing the masses. In our efforts to influence the middle class for Christ, we need to consider new ministries to serve women.

Endnotes

*** K. John Amalraj**, Bachelor of Law, MA in Political Science, PG Dip in Human Resources, Master of Divinity (Trinity Theological College, Singapore). He was Executive Secretary and National Director, Interserve India at the time of this consultation.

**** Lunkhomang Haokip,** Bachelor of Arts (Manipur University), Master of Theology (Missiology) from Union Biblical Seminary, Pune. He was a Research Coordinator at Interserve India during this consultation.

[1] J.N. Manokaran, *Christ and Cities: Transformation of Urban Cultures* (Chennai: Mission Educational Books, 2005), 53.

[2] K. Rajendran, *Which Way Forward Indian Missions? A Critique of Twenty-five Years 1972 – 1997* (Bangalore: SAIACS Press, 1998), 36.

[3] B.B. Misra, *The Indian Middle Classes: Their Growth in Modern Times* (Delhi: Oxford University Press, 1961), 12.

[4] Pavan K. Varma, *The Great Indian Middle Class* (New Delhi: Penguin Books India, Pvt.Ltd., 1998), xviii.

[5] John Amalraj, "Survey of a Changing World," in *Where are the Indian Leaders? Developing Leadership in Indian Missions,* ed.K. Rajendran and John Amalraj (Chennai: India Mission Association, 2000), 24.

6 Diana Farrell and Eric Beinhocker, "Next Big Spenders: India's Middle Class," *Newsweek International* May 19,2007, http://www.mckinsey.com/mgi/mginews/bigspenders.asp.

7 Adite Chatterjee, "The New Market Place," *Business Today,* February 1996, 83.

8 R. Lewis and A. Maude, *The English Middle Classes* cited in Bhagwan Prasad, *Socio-Economic Study of Urban Middle Classes* (Delhi: Sterling Publishers, 1968), 6.

9 Atul Y. Aghamkar, *"Approaching Urban Hindus: A Study of Christian Approaches and Hindu Responses in Pune City, India"* (PhD diss., Fuller Theological Seminary, 1995), 78.

10 Misra, *The Indian Middle Classes,* 10.

11 Varma, *The Great Indian Middle Class* , xxiii.

12 Farrell and Beinhocker, "Next Big Spenders."

13 Misra, *Indian Middle Class,* 11.

14 David H. Wells, "Milestones: A Road Map to the Indian Middle Class" APF Reporter 20, no. 1 (2001), accessed March 5, 2010, http://www.aliciapatterson.org/APF2001/Wells.html.

15 Rajendran, *Which Way Forward Indian Missions?,* 37.

16 Lunkhomang Haokip, "Survey of the Indian Middle Class in the Context of Five Selected Cities of India", in *Walking the Way of The Cross: With our Hindu Friends,* ed. Ellen Alexender and Robin Thomson (Bangalore: Primalogue Publishing Media Private Limited, 2011), 167 – 176.

17 Zakir Naik, *Concept of God in Hinduism,* accessed March 5,2010, http://saif_w.tripod.com/interfaith/general/god/inhinduism.htm.

18 "Concept of God in Islam," *WAMY Series: On Islam* No.9, accessed March 5,2010, http://www.sultan.org/articles/god.html.

19 *"Concept of God in Jainism," accessed March 5, 2010,* http://www.jainuniversity.org/jainism_god.aspx

20 "Buddhists Concept of God and Gods,"accessed March 5, 2010, http://www.knowbuddhism.info/2009/03/buddhists-concept-of-god-and-gods.html".

21 "Concept of God in Sikh Religion," accessed March 5, 2010, http://religion.indianetzone.com/1/concept_god_sikh_religion.htm.

[22] "Atheist" | Dictionary.com. accessed March 5, 2010, http://dictionary. reference.com/browse/atheist.

[23] J. Andrew Kirk, *What is Mission?: Theological Explorations* (London: Darton, Longman & Todd, 1999), 128.

Bibliography

Aghamkar, Atul Y. "Approaching Urban Hindus: A Study of Christian Approaches and Hindu Responses in Pune City, India." PhD diss., Fuller Theological Seminary, 1995.

Amalraj, John. "Survey of a Changing World." In *Where Are the Indian Leaders? Developing Indian Leadership in Indian Missions*, edited by K. Rajendran and John Amalraj, 19 - 28. Chennai: Indian Missions Association, 2004.

"Atheist." *Dictionary.com*. https://www.dictionary.com/browse/atheist.

"Buddhists Concept of God and Gods," n.d. http://www.knowbuddhism. info/2009/03/ buddhists-concept-of-god-and-gods.html.

Chatterjee, Adite. "The New Marketplace." *Business Today*, February 1996.

"Concept of God in Islam." http://www.sultan.org/articles/god.html.

"Concept of God in Jainism," n.d. http://www.jainuniversity. org/jainism_ god.aspx.

"Concept of God in Sikh Religion," n.d. http://religion.indianetzone.com/1/ concept_god_sikh_religion.htm.

Farrell, Diana and Eric Beinhocker. "Next Big Spenders: India's Middle Class." *McKinsey Global Institute*, May 19, 2007. https://www.mckinsey.com/ mgi/overview/in-the-news/next-big-spenders-indian-middle-class.

Haokip, Lunkhomang. "Survey of the Indian Middle Class in the Context of Five Selected Cities of India." In *Walking the Way of the Cross: With Our Hindu Friends*. Edited by Ellen Alexander, and Robin Thomson, 167–76. Bangalore: Primalogue Publishing Media Private Limited, 2011.

Kirk, J. Andrew. *What is Mission? : Theological Explorations*. London: Darton, Longman & Todd, 1999.

Lewis, Roy and Angus Maude. *The English Middle Classes*. Chivers, 1973.

Manokaran, J. N. *Christ & Cities: Transformation of Urban Centers*. Chennai: Mission Educational Books, 2005.

Misra, Bankey Bihari. *The Indian Middle Classes: Their Growth in Modern Times*. Oxford University Press, 1961.

Naik, Zakir. "Concept of God in Hinduism." http://saif_w.tripod.com/interfaith/general/god/inhinduism.htm.

Prasad, Bhagwan. *Socio-Economic Study of Urban Middle Class*. Delhi: Sterling Publisher Private Ltd., 1968.

Rajendran, K. *Which Way Forward Indian Missions? A Critique of Twenty-Five Years, 1972-1997*. Bangalore: SAIACS Press, 1998.

Varma, Pavan K. *The Great Indian Middle Class*. New Delhi: Penguin Books India, 1998.

Wells, David H. "Milestones: A Road Map to the Indian Middle Class." *APF Reporter* 20, no. 1 (2001). http://www.aliciapatterson.org/APF2001/Wells.html.

CHAPTER - 2

The Middle Class in India and Some Lessons from the Bible on Reaching Them

*J. N. Manokaran**

Introduction

The empirical research done by Interserve on four cities shows that the religious and spiritual quest among the middle class is shown in the increase in the number of people visiting temples, doing charity, downloading spiritual music and discourses from internet, increase in the number of exclusive religious satellite tv channels and space in print media. The need for spiritual opening of their minds is real; the quest for truth is evident but the challenge to the Church in India is to formulate relevant, convincing, creative and contextual strategy for communicating the gospel to the urban middle class. However, a brief survey of the missiological literature suggests that urban leaders around the world in missions have focused on the poor. Viv Grigg argues that the gospel is primarily for the poor according to Nazareth Manifesto.[1] Patrick Johnstone writes that the urban poor are the most receptive, most under evangelized and are about 40 per cent of the city population.[2] He also fails to bring in focus the 60 per cent who among them are urban middle class also. Larry L. Rose and C. Kirk Hadaway have edited a book, *An Urban World,* which provides the need for reaching the cities. Here also the focus seems to be poor of the cities.[3] George A. Torney has compiled a book on urban strategy, where the focus is urban poor and unchurched people.[4] Murray H. Leiffer writes about the American churches reaching the inner cities that are cities within the cities.[5] Some authors have written about the cults in the city, migrants in the city but mostly focus on the poor; *Cites and Churches: Reading on the Urban Church*, is a good example.[6] Jenni M. Craig has documented ministries among the poor in the cities.[7] The Incarnational model among the poor is stressed in the book, *God So Loves the City*.[8] Prompted by this deficiency this essay is a humble attempt to expose stories from the Bible where the well-to-do people were reached.

This essay is composed of three parts. Firstly, it deals with the emergence of the middle class in India. Secondly, it exposes the challenges of middle class for Christian missionaries. Thirdly, it exposes some Bible characters who are considered in this essay as middle class and the witness to them. An extended study of these character can help in strategizing to propel mission to the emerging middle class in India.

Emergence of Middle Class in India

Pre-Independence

It is not the industrial revolution that gave birth to middle class in India but colonial rule of the British. Unlike America and Europe, Indian urban middle class has its root in the British Raj. Misra writes that the ideas and institutions of a middle-class social order were imported into India by the British and did not emerge from within. They were transplanted in the country without a comparable development in its economy and social institutions. The British wanted the Indian middle class to be a class of imitators, not the originators of new values and methods.[9] Until that time the caste was the real identity of a person that had religious sanction. "According to the most prevalent belief, the Brahmins, Kshatriyas, Vaishyas and Shudras are said to have been separately created from the mouth, the arms, the thighs and the feet respectively of the creator-the god."[10] The British challenged this concept as they created a new class especially in the urban administrative centers. The British introduction of new order that stood for intellectual freedom, social mobility, liberal individualism and political democracy created a new value for individual apart from religious sanction of authority which was caste.[11] "The creation of a native elite in its own image was the most spectacular and enduring achievement of British colonialism in India."[12]

In India, it was the political environment of colonization which created a new class of people who enjoyed not political power but political patronage that created the middle class. "In the British period, Indian cities became the focal points of westernization. Schools, colleges and universities trained men and women in western thought and languages. A new western oriented urban elite emerged."[13] There was also social factor, the upper Castes were more mobile and agile to use the opportunities offered by the British to move into British creation of middle class. The influence of British created middle classes from a variety of backgrounds. The rural landlords became rich farmers. The educated middle class was the beneficiary of the English education introduced by the missionaries and the British Raj.

In British Raj there were officials, businessmen and banking houses that formed the middle class. They were called as commercial middle class.[14] They were rich farmers, elite educated, commercial, technical and government servants who formed the middle class in the British Raj. "In the British period, Indian cities became the focal points of westernization. Schools, colleges and universities trained men and women in western thought and languages. A new western oriented urban elite emerged."[15]

Dipankar Gupta writes, "Caste and class both bring to our minds inequality and hierarchy."[16] While caste was rigid religious social order where upward mobility was very limited, class opened doors for upward mobility. According to Srinivas who disagrees with Gupta, a low caste was able, in a generation or two, to rise to a higher position in hierarchy by adopting vegetarianism and teetotalism, and by Sanskritizing its ritual and pantheon. In short, it took over, as far as possible, the customs, rites, and beliefs of the Brahmins, and the adoption of Brahminic way of life by a low caste seems to have been frequent, though forbidden. This process is called "Sanskritization".[17] In fact, this process gained momentum under the British Raj. "The spread of Sanskrit theological ideas increased under British rule. The development of communications carried Sanskritization to areas previously inaccessible, and the spread of literacy carried it to groups very low in the caste hierarchy."[18] The political environment created by the British, created a group of people who became middle class with English education, at the same time the people of low caste also climbed up by adopting Brahminical way of life of vegetarianism and teetotalism and getting English education into middle class bandwagon.

Post 1990

For the first time in India's history, a sizeable and increasingly homogenous bourgeoisie is emerging. The market driven global liberal economy dominating India, there is convergence of middle class from different background. This class knows only too well that access to education is essential to retain their hard won economic and social gains and domination. The competition for obtaining access to higher education, in particular, medical, engineering and technological courses, is likely to increase in the immediate future as such courses has status value besides being lucrative.[19] "The urban population in India has a greater proportion of literates and degree holders."[20]

The political environment of British Raj created a bureaucratic middle class under political patronage. The Railways and other industries also created an industrial middle class before Independence. The Post – Independence era with the thrust for industrialization under Jawaharlal Nehru saw an increase in the industrial middle class. The economic reforms has brought sea change in several aspects of Indian life and it is considered irreversible. "A new middle class emerges a decade after the launch of economic reforms. Peopled by a different breed of entrepreneurs and consumers, it is street savvy, uninhibited and pragmatic."[21] The economic reforms added up a new economic middle class. The educated, articulate and the upward mobile with post-modern attitude are dominating the urban life today. They embrace the new "Information Era" and look forward to have a slice of global economic pie.

Terming income as an indicator, then middle class can be defined as a household with an income of Rs. 12000 per annum. If a household earns a monthly income of less than Rs. 12 000, that household is not middle class. That household is poor. "According to the National Council for Applied Economic Research (NCAER), a family with an annual income between Rs. 3.4 lakh to Rs. 17 lakh (at 2009-10 price levels) falls in the middle class category. According to NCAER, by 2015-16, India will be a country of 53.3 million middle class households or about 267 million people."[22]

Challenge of Indian Middle Class

The Church in India has the mandate as the part of universal global church to fulfil the Great Commission task of communicating the gospel. The middle class community is a new mosaic in the cities that have not responded enthusiastically and positively to the gospel.

The influential thinking class of the country is increasingly favouring the *Hindutva* political ideology. BJP has firmly established as the party of the aspiring middle classes.[23] It is essential to win the minds of people for Christ so that the whole nation may be transformed.

The urban middle class are strategic people or 'gate way' people, who can communicate and demonstrate the power of gospel to the whole nation. The Church by initiating the ministry among them would usher the Kingdom of God in a powerful way. This study would help to understand the aspirations and mind set of urban middle class. Which in turn would reveal the 'felt needs' of the people. By meeting such needs, the Church could plan evangelism strategies to reach them.

The Church in India has made attempts in the history, as well as in the present context to reach the thinking, educated and non-poor. But there is a great scope of reaching the city middle class in India. "A report by National Council for Applied Economic Research's (NCAER) Centre for Macro Consumer

Research said by 2015-16, India will be a country of 53.3 million middle class households, translating into 267 million people falling in the category."[24] This gives a greater challenge in terms of numbers for mission efforts in the coming day.

Biblical Accounts of Reaching the Well-to-do

The first century church history as recorded in the Acts of Apostles by Luke states that all people in the society were reached with the gospel. All classes of the society: The elite, the middle class and the poor responded to the gospel message.

> If Lydia came from the top end of the social scale and the slave girl from the bottom, the Roman Jailer was one of the sturdy middle class who made up the Roman Civil Service; and so, in these three the whole range within the society was complete.[25]

The gospel is for the whole society comprising all classes, ethnicity and language.

Theophilus

People in the Empire of Rome were divided into two major classes. The upper class consisted of emperors, senators, knights and wealthy individuals of local councils; the lower class: Citizens with privilege, non-citizens without privilege and slaves.[26] Luke audience was considered as cosmopolitan and middle-class:

> Saint Luke wrote for an audience quite different from those of Mark and Matthew, different, too, from the Thessalonians and many other recipients of Paul's letters. Luke's readers lived a generation or more later than the apostles, after the destruction of Jerusalem by the Romans in 70 C.E., and outside the Holy Land. They had never been Jews. They were cosmopolitan, middle-class and Gentile, living in a skeptical society, yet attracted to a religion with long historic Jewish roots.[27]

Luke addresses both the gospel of Luke and the Acts of Apostles to Theophilus. "The Gospel of Luke is addressed to Theophilus with the expression: "most excellent Theophilus."[28] This phrasing indicates that Theophilus was a Roman official."[29] Luke was a medical professional and had journalistic capacity and skills. He had the intellectual capacity to write to a Roman official who was another middle class intellectual. Theophilus could have been at par with the Civil Service official (Indian Administrative Service) in India today. Literature is an important tool used by the first century church to introduce the gospel to educated middle class. Luke was a writer who could address a contemporary intellectual and professional.

Day of Pentecost

The disciples after ascension of Lord Jesus Christ gathered in the Upper Room. The number of people gathered is recorded as 120. Since Lord Jesus Christ was crucified, the disciples could not have got a public hall to tarry for the Holy Spirit. They needed a place to gather a group of 120 people. As some evidences show that it was the home of John Mark and his mother Mary. John Mark must have been brought up in a rich environment and most probably not able to undergo tedious missionary journey along with Paul and Barnabas.

> John Mark also was surrounded with Christian influence in his teen years. He might have met Jesus as He came in for His last Passover with His disciples. After the Ascension of the Lord Jesus the disciples returned to the upper room for a prayer meeting (Acts 1:12-14). The house seems to be one of the places where the early church gathered in Jerusalem.[30]

The middle class and upper class disciples of Lord Jesus Christ ministered by providing infrastructure and material needs.

> After this, Jesus travelled about from one town and village to another, proclaiming the good news of the kingdom of God. The Twelve were with him, and also some women who had been cured of evil spirits and diseases: Mary (called Magdalene) from whom seven demons had come out; Joanna the wife of Chuza, the manager of Herod's household; Susanna; and many others. These women were helping to support them out of their own means.[31]

Simon the Sorcerer

Philip goes to Samaria to preach the gospel. Simon the sorcerer was so impressed by the miracles done by Philip. He discerned that the power of these people was through the Person of Holy Spirit. So, he was willing to pay money for getting the power to dispense Holy Spirit. Peter rebukes him.[32] The sorcerer was economically well off to offer money in exchange of a spiritual gift. Philip takes the gospel to the city of Samaria, where the middle class also responded to his message. Philip was led by the Spirit of God into the wilderness. There he meets the Ethiopian eunuch who oversaw the treasury of Kandake (which means queen of Ethiopians).[33] He was reading from the Book of Isaiah but could not understand. Philip explains the passage and shares how the prophet was speaking about Lord Jesus Christ the Messiah. The finance secretary or minister of Ethiopia was baptized by Philip. A lay leader of the Jerusalem church ministers to the finance minister of Ethiopia. The Ethiopian minister is certainly from middle class or even upper class.

Tabitha, a Philanthropist

Dorcas alias Tabitha in city of Joppa was helping the poor generously.[34] A person who could be able to help so many poor people should have been from a wealthy background. The wealthy middle class Tabitha was not only a disciple but was willing to help and serve the poor.

Cornelius of Italian Regiment

Peter was reluctant to take the gospel to Cornelius and had to be guided by our Lord through a trance. Cornelius was prepared to receive the gospel by the visit of an angel. Cornelius was a centurion – an important high official in the Italian Regiment.[35] Army officers in the Roman Empire were accorded high status in the society.

Manaen, Royal Household

Manaen, who was brought up with Herod the tetrarch was one of the five leaders of the Antioch church.[36] He is considered as the foster brother of Herod. This person was from royal background and was a middle class in the Roman Empire.

Antioch Church Commissions Missionaries

The Church at Antioch was able to commission Saul and Barnabas as missionaries. The middle class in the Roman Empire were mobile and they travelled.

> During the time of Augustus, for the first time it was relatively safe for people to travel and people enjoyed travelling, much as Americans began to travel after the middle class were able to acquire automobiles. As a result, trade expanded throughout the Mediterranean world. Apostle Paul's missionary journeys are a good testimony indicating that the middle class travelled widely throughout the Roman Empire.[37]

Sergus Paulus, Proconsul

Sergus Paulus was a Proconsul in Paphos, Cyprus who believed Lord Jesus Christ through the preaching of Paul.[38]

> A proconsul was a governor of a province in the Roman Republic appointed for one year by the senate. In modern usage, the title has been used (sometimes disparagingly) for a person from one country ruling another country or bluntly interfering in another country's internal affairs."[39]

Timothy

Timothy was born of cross-cultural marriage lived in the city of Derbe.[40] Marriage of a Jewess to a Greek person was a rare occurrence. Since, father of Timothy was from middle class, there may not have been much opposition to this marriage. Timothy was well educated including Jewish scripture means that the family belonged to middle class of Roman Empire. Hence, Timothy fits in as an urban Pastor. Interreligious marriages happen among the middle class in urban centres. Children of such marriages should be open to the gospel.

Lydia, a Dealer of Purple Cloth

Lydia was most likely a Greek even though she lived in a Roman settlement. She was evidently a well-to-do agent of a purple-dye firm in Thyatira, a city southeast of Pergamum and approximately 40 miles inland, across the Aegean Sea from Athens.[41]

Lydia was a prominent businesswoman.[42] Lydia's customers were rich, wealthy and nobles – ruling class. Lydia was wealthy that she was able to accommodate Paul and his team in her home. In the modern times, Lydia was like a high profile businesswoman marketing high end products for the rich.

Jailer

Paul and Silas were arrested for preaching the gospel. The jailed apostles praised and worshipped the Lord. There was an earthquake and the two men of God had an opportunity to escape. The Jailer was about to kill himself while Paul called out to him that they are available and not run away. Jailer and his household were baptized.[43] Jailer was a security office like Inspector General of Prisons. The Jailer was from middle class and was like an Indian Police Service (IPS) officer.

Athens – Aeropagus

Athens was a city where intellectuals and philosophers met, discussed and debated various theories, ideas and philosophies. "The Areopagus, or "Hill of Ares" (Ἀρεῖος πάγος), in Athens was the site of a council that served as an important legal institution under the Athenian democracy."[44] Paul was able to proclaim the gospel to the elite – educated, rich and powerful in Athens. "Some of the people became followers of Paul and believed. Among them was Dionysius, a member of the Areopagus, also a woman named Damaris, and a number of others."[45] This is like speaking to the elected members of city council or senate of a university.

Aquila and Priscilla

Aquila and Priscilla were tentmaking professionals.[46] Tentmaking means to provide shelters or homes for the people. The couple were non-citizens but were wealthy enough to relocate and continue the business. They are similar to the people involved in real estate business.

Paul, Global Nomad

Paul was a Roman citizen by birth.[47] He was elite that he could afford to study under great teacher Gamaliel.[48] He communicated in Greek, then the global language for communication and power.

Publius

Publius was the Chief official of the Island of Malta.[49] His father was sick, Paul prayed and healed him. Certainly, Publius was a Middle Class in the Roman Empire and also wealthy. Paul reaches him with the Gospel.

To Paul, as to all of the apostles, the gospel was primary, and culture was secondary. Gentiles did not have to adopt the Jewish culture to be saved for the gospel did not require it. Neither Jews nor Gentiles were compelled to forsake their culture, as long as the gospel was not compromised by it. Whenever the gospel could be promoted by adapting to the culture of another, the preaching of the gospel required such change. In addition to the implications of the gospel which govern culture, culture is also an important consideration because of its impact on the gospel.[50]

Conclusion

Christianity in India has a history of nearly 2000 years. But the Christian presence and influence is miniscule and largely among the under privileged of the society. Somehow, the gospel has not been presented as a vibrant option to the rich and the thinking intelligentsia of this country. The upper class, middle class and intelligentsia that are educated, articulates and influences the thought process and shapes the future of this country. This includes the academicians, artists, media personnel, philosophers, scientists, finance managers, economists, lawyers, politicians, etc. In the new information Age, the middle class are everywhere seen and heard. They are trendsetters in lifestyle, role models in economic sphere, leaders in political opinion and set agenda for the nation. There is a yearning for Christians to see these people become disciples of Lord Jesus Christ and lead a "Christ-ward" transformation movement in this nation. This essay has identified fifteen biblical characters who provide lessons on reaching the middle class in India.

Endnotes

* **Dr. J. N. Manokaran** is a civil engineer by profession. He was serving as the Managing Director of Trainers of Pastors International Coalition, at the time of this Consultation.

[1] Viv Grigg, *Cry of the Urban Poor* (Marc, 2000), 10.

[2] Patrick Johnstone, *The Church is Bigger Than You Think* (Pasadena: William Carey Library, 2000), 241-248.

[3] Larry L. Rose and C. Kirk Hadaway, ed., *An Urban World: Churches Face the Future* (Nashville: Broadman Press, 1984).

[4] George A. Torney, ed., *Toward Creative Urban Strategy* (Taco: Word Book Publisher, 1970).

[5] Murray H. Leiffer, *The Effective City Church* (New York: Abington Press, 1961).

[6] Robert Lee, ed., *Cities and Churches: Reading on the Urban Church* (Philadelphia: The Westminster Press, n.d.).

[7] Jenni M. Craig, *Servants among the Poor* (Manila: OMF Literature, 1997).

[8] Charles Van Engen and Jude Tiersma, ed., *God So Loves the City* (MARC 1994).

[9] B. B. Misra, *The Indian Middle Classes their Growth in Modern Times* (London: Oxford University Press, 1983), 11.

[10] Shyam S. Agarwalla, *Religion & Caste Politics* (Jaipur & New Delhi Rawat: Publications, 1998), 132.

[11] Misra, *The Indian Middle Classes their Growth in Modern Times*, 7.

[12] Pavan K. Varma, *The Great Indian Middle Class* (New Delhi: Penguin Books, 1998), 2.

[13] R. Ramachandran, *Urbanization and Urban Systems in India* (New Delhi, Oxford University Press, 2001), 69.

[14] Misra, *The Indian Middle Classes their Growth in Modern Times*, 77-78

[15] R. Ramachandran, *Urbanization and Urban Systems in India* (New Delhi, Oxford University Press, 2001), 69.

[16] Dipankar Gupta, *Social Stratification* (Bombay: Oxford University Press, 1991), 9.

[17] Srinivas, *Caste in Modern India*, 42.

[18] Srinivas, *Caste in Modern India*, 48.

[19] Srinivas, *Caste in Modern India*, 476.

[20] Ramachandran, *Urbanization and Urban Systems in India*, 103.

[21] Matthew, "Letter from the Chief Editor," *The Week*, (December 30, 2001), 4.

[22] V. N. Mukundarajan, *Why Make the Middle Class the Whipping Boy?* accessed on November 4, 2011. *http://www.thehindu.com/opinion/open-page/article2580553.ece.*

[23] John Micklethwait, "In God's Name," *The Economist,* (November 3, 2007), 14.

[24] "India's Middle Class to Touch 267 Million in 5 Years," *The Economic Time,* February 6, 2011, accessed on January 10, 2012, http://articles.economictimes.indiatimes.com/2011-02-06/news/28424975_1_middle-class-households-applied-economic-research.

[25] William Barclay, *The Acts of Apostles* (Louisville, London: Westminster John Knox Press, 2003)

[26] "Class and Rank in the Roman Empire," *American Bible Society: Resources,* accessed January 10, 2012, http://bibleresources.americanbible.org/bible-resources/bible-resource-center/about-the-bible-/behind-the-stories/class-and-rank-roman-empire.

[27] "Lector's Notes," accessed October 25, 2011, http://www.lectorprep.org/easter_03_yrB.html.

[28] Luke 1:3.

[29] Ronald l. Conte, Jr., "The Writing of the New Testament – Luke and Acts," *Catholic Planet: Roman Catholic Theology and Biblical Studies,* accessed December 22, 2011, http://www.catholicplanet.com/TSM/NT-Luke.htm.

[30] Gordon Franz, "John Mark: Always Playing Second Fiddle," *Profiles in Missions,* accessed January 15, 2012, http://ldolphin.org/johnmark.html.

[31] Luke 8:1-3 (New International Version).

[32] Acts 8:9-24.

[33] Acts 8:27.

[34] Acts 9:38.

[35] Acts 10:1.

[36] Acts 13:1.

[37] "1. Emergence of the Middle Class and Specialization," *World Possibility Productivity Centre,* accessed on January 5, 2012, http://www2.econ.iastate.edu/classes/econ355/choi/ric2.htm.

[38] Acts 13:12.

[39] "Proconsul," *Wikipedia: The Free Encyclopedia,* accessed 12 January 2012, http://en.wikipedia.org/wiki/Proconsul.

40 Acts 16:1-3.

41 "Lydia of Thyatira," *Wikipedia: The Free Encyclopedia*, accessed January 12, 2012, http://en.wikipedia.org/wiki/Lydia_of_Thyatira.

42 Acts 16:14-15.

43 Acts 16:29-30.

44 "The Council of the Areopagus," *Demos*, accessed January 12, 2012, http://www.stoa.org/projects/demos/article_areopagus?page=all&greekEncoding=UnicodeC.

45 Acts 17:34.

46 Acts 18:1-3.

47 Acts 22: 25-28.

48 Acts 22:3.

49 Acts 28:7.

50 Bob Deffinbaugh, "3. Cults, Christianity, and Culture (Acts 15:1-31)," *Bible.org*, accessed October 25, 2011, http://bible.org/seriespage/cults-christianity-and-culture-acts-151-31.

Bibliography

"Emergence of the Middle Class and Specialization." *World Possibility Productivity Centre.* http://www2.econ.iastate.edu/classes/econ355/choi/ric2.htm.

"Class and Rank in the Roman Empire." *American Bible Society: Resources.* http://bibleresources.americanbible.org/bible-resources/bible-resource-center/about-the-bible-/behind-the-stories/class-and-rank-roman-empire.

"India's Middle Class to Touch 267 Million in 5 Years." http://articles.economictimes.indiatimes.com/2011-02-06/news/28424975_1_middle-class-households-applied-economic-research.

"Lector's Notes." http://www.lectorprep.org/easter_03_yrB.html.

"Lydia of Thyatira." *Wikipedia: The Free Encyclopedia.* http://en.wikipedia.org/wiki/Lydia_of_Thyatira.

"Proconsul." *Wikipedia: The Free Encyclopedia.* http://en.wikipedia.org/wiki/Proconsul.

"The Council of the Areopagus." *Demos.* (http://www.stoa.org/projects/demos/article_areopagus?page=all&greekEncoding=UnicodeC.

Agarwalla, Shyam S. *Religion & Caste Politics*. Jaipur & New Delhi: Rawat Publications, 1998.

Barclay, William. *The Acts of Apostles*. Louisville, London: Westminster John Knox Press, 2003.

Conte, Ronald Jr. "The Writing of the New Testament – Luke and Acts." *Catholic Planet: Roman Catholic Theology and Biblical Studies*. http:// www.catholicplanet.com/TSM/NT-Luke.htm.

Craig, Jenni M. *Servants among the Poor*. Manila: OMF Literature, 1997.

Dalrymple, William. *Nine Lives in Search of Sacred in Modern India*. London: Bloomsbury Publication Plc, 2009.

Das, Gurcharan. *The Elephant Paradigm: India Wrestles with Change*. New Delhi: Penguin Publications India, 2001.

Deffinbaugh, Bob. "3. Cults, Christianity, and Culture (Acts 15:1-31)." *Bible.org*. http://bible.org/seriespage/cults-christianity-and-culture-acts-151-31.

Engen, Charles Van and Jude Tiersma, ed. *God So Loves the City*. MARC 1994.

Franz, Gordon. *John Mark: Always Playing Second Fiddle*. http://ldolphin. org/johnmark.html.

Grenz, Stanley J. *A Primer on Postmodernism*. Grand Rapids: William B Eerdmans Publishing Company, 1996.

Grigg, Viv. *Cry of the Urban Poor*. Marc, 2000.

Gupta, Dipankar. *Social Stratification*. Bombay: Oxford University Press, 1991.

Gupta, Sanjiv. "Great Indian Buyers." *The Week*. December 30, 2001.

http://www.gospelcom.net/lcwe/statements/manila.html

Johnstone, Patrick. *The Church is Bigger Than You Think*. Pasadena: William Carey Library, 2000.

Lee, Robert, ed. *Cities and Churches: Reading on the Urban Church*. Philadelphia: The Westminster Press, n.d.

Leiffer, Murray H. *The Effective City Church*. New York: Abington Press, 1961.

Matthew, Mammen. "Letter from The Chief Editor." *The Week*. December 30, 2001.

Micklethwait, John. "In God's Name." *The Economist*. November 3, 2007.

Misra, B. B. *The Indian Middle Classes their Growth in Modern Times*. London: Oxford University Press, 1983.

Mukundarajan, V. N. *Why Make the Middle Class the Whipping Boy? http:// www.thehindu.com/opinion/open-page/article2580553.ece*

Ramachandran, R. *Urbanization and Urban Systems in India*. New Delhi, Oxford University Press, 2001.

Rose, Larry L. and C. Kirk Hadaway, ed. *An Urban World: Churches Face the Future*. Nashville: Broadman Press, 1984.

Sjoberg, Gideon. *The Preindustrial City: Past and Present*. New York: The Free Press, 1965.

Srinivas, M. N. *Caste in Modern India*. Bombay: Media Promoters & Publishers Pvt. Ltd., 1998.

The Holy Bible. New International Version.

Toffler, Alvin. *The Third Wave*. London: Pan Books Limited, 1981.

Torney, George A., ed. *Toward Creative Urban Strategy*. Taco: Word Book Publisher, 1970.

Tully, Mark *India's Unending Journey: Finding Balance in a Time of Change*. London: Rider, 2007.

Varma, Pavan K. *The Great Indian Middle Class*. New Delhi: Penguin Books, 1998.

CHAPTER - 3

Contemporary Middle Class Youth in India: Challenges and Opportunities for the Church

*John M. Prasad**

Introduction

The Middle class always existed and they exist all over the world. However, the changing global scene, has initiated a process of transformation in the middle class. This transformation is leading the middle class to a new set of values and behaviour with inherent tension between the traditional values of the class and the global values, both of which the class is unwilling to part with. This is leading the middle class to a split-level identity, traditional at times and modern at other times. The segment of the middle class population that leads the way for the middle class is the urban youth members of the class. Some of the key words that can describe this urban middle class youth are opportunity, competition, survival, consumerism, entertainment and extravaganza.

Most of the scholars agree that the number of middle class is rapidly increasing in India. The global market is seeing a business opportunity in the middle class who are believed to be spenders and not those who preserve or save. The business also seeks to exploit their opportunity by adding fuel to the spending habit of the new and upcoming middle class. The phenomenal growth of the middle class is not resulting from inheritance. Rather it is because of the elevation of the large number of the underprivileged to the middle class segment as a result of their hard work and determination. As the number of middle class is increasing significantly in India, they become a major percentage of the population. Moreover, the contemporary middle class appears to develop a pan-Indian unique culture and identity, with its own forms of responding to challenges and opportunities. We will also be able to trace a typical way the members of the contemporary middle class respond to religion and thus also to the gospel. The mission movements in India cannot ignore this growing class of the Indian society as a special group which calls for strategy aimed at making the gospel to have an impact in their lives.

Who are the Middle Class?

The definition of middle class cannot be very simple and objective. There are widely varying definitions to mark the category of middle class. The most common criteria for defining the middle class category is by the family income, though this may not be the only criteria. Rukmini Srinivasan defines middle class thus;

> In socio-political terms, the middle class is traditionally that segment of society with a degree of economic security that allows it to uphold the rule of law, invest and desire stability. They do not, unlike those defined as rich, depend on inheritances or other non-productive sources of income.[1]

The Interserve India Survey has taken the economic criteria and has defined those with a family income of Rs 20,000 and above as the middle class. The Survey does not specify the upper limit of the income. Thus, it is not clear where the upper class is distinguished from the middle class. Srinivasan further refer to the study of Nancy Birdsall which was to be published in a World Bank publication in which she gives a new definition for the middle class in developing countries.

> Birdsall defines the middle class in the developing world to include people with an income above $10 day, but excluding the top 5% of that country. By this definition, India even urban India alone has no middle class; everyone at over $10 a day is in the top 5% of the country.[2]

Apparently, for our purpose, a definition of the middle class in India has to be India specific and the economic criteria cannot be compared with that of other countries, especially developed countries. Pavan Varma in his classic work[3] do not attempt to give an objective definition of the middle class but assumes that the reader has a definition of the middle class, which is a combination of economic index, lifestyle, purchasing power, economic security and a culture of its own. This also leads to Indian middle class to have a unique identity of its own, different from other identities based on religion, caste, tribe, or language.

The Emerging Middle Class Youth in India

The middle class in India has been going through radical transformation over the last few decades. Whatever we will discuss further is more applicable to the youth and the middle-aged members of the middle class. Varma traces the big transformation to the economic liberalization that started in 1991.[4] He candidly narrates the multi-dimensional transformation that has happened with the middle class. We can reasonably conclude that this transformation also has led them to a middle class identity as well as a contemporary middle class culture. Varma points out that,

> As the size of the economic cake grew, so did the jobs and business opportunities for middle class Indians. The IT boom at the turn of the millennium was a sponge for the thousands of technically trained graduates produced by the expanding network of higher education institutions.[5]

There are several levels of transformation that took place among the middle class during this period. The main observations by Varma can be summarized as follows.

1. The number of the middle class began to swell since the economic reforms of 1991. The new members of the class are drawn from all categories and walks of life, thus bringing heterogeneity to the class itself.

2. The heterogeneity also is coupled with "an easily identifiable underlying homogeneity." The new identity of the middle class is strengthened by the new connectivity globally and nationally, through social media, television and other means.

3. Gandhian ideals of austerity and Nehruvian socialism are no longer ideals of the contemporary middle class youth.

4. There is "more money and more things that money can buy." Thus, consumerism has come to the heart of the contemporary middle class youth.[6]

5. Education is the key factor that is the tool for the middle class to seize the opportunities to climb the economic ladder up. This is demonstrated in the mushrooming of institutions of vocational education and the tremendous

amount of effort that is put by the middle class into acquiring higher education.

6. There is a universal "aspiration for affluence" among all classes in India, once the poor "climb the ladder on to the middle class bandwagon or higher", they are insensitive to those who are left behind. Thus, the middle class exhibit a certain level of separation from the poor and become insensitive to their plight. This leads to a situation where the deprived are all the more deprived and often left in despair.[7]

7. The contemporary middle class has a strong influence on the government and policy as they are more vocal and united at national level in what they see as a threat to their prospects. Thus, we see agitation against corruption, crime etc. moving powerfully with the middle class strength, while there is hardly any middle class movement to save the poor.

8. Religion and secularism are both cherished and frowned upon as the middle class struggle with the tension between the two. They are hesitant to give up either.[8]

Some of the observations of Varma are supported in the Interserve survey which indicates the attitude of the middle class to various concerns mentioned above. 82% of those surveyed in the study are between the age group of 25 and 40. The study was limited to the ten urban centers and hence is primarily representative of the urban middle class youth only. While we can claim that the middle class are primarily concentrated in the cities, there can be no clue to the social and religious attitude of the middle class from rural contexts if at all those who fall within the definition of middle class are to be found in rural contexts too. Similarly, 87% of the respondents had education at university level, a level of education that shifts their identity to a different class. We need to find out what percentage of those who were interviewed were migrants from rural contexts for the sake of education or employment.

We can also see that 87% of those who were studied were employed in professions that depend on other agencies such as government, an institution or a company. Again, we can see that 80% of those who were interviewed were in the income bracket up to Rs 41,667, that is the two lower slabs. The same percentage is repeated in most of the questions on the personal information section. 86% of them felt that they will view their economic status as middle class.

Coming to the questions of the religious experience and the perspective of God, the tension between the secular and the religious views are visible. There is almost equal divide between a personal experience of God and the concept of God as something non-personal. The divine is not necessarily personal, rather more a power or force. The divide is almost close to 40% and 40% in each of the groups. This proportion is also seen in many responses about personal relationship with God, or prayer or sin and salvation etc. Here is where we find the struggle of the contemporary middle class between their desire to be rich and material prosperity and the spiritual values cherished and exalted traditionally.

What is rather surprising here is the percentage of people who responded to the question on the person and work of Jesus Christ. Though the number of Christians in the interview could be anywhere less than 1%, the number of those who responded that salvation is possible through the blood of Jesus Christ is a surprising 9%. There is a further 29% of the respondents who agreed with Christians who claim that Jesus is the only way to salvation. These responses need to be further verified. However, if that stands to be an accurate picture of how the non-Christians feel about the claim of Christians about salvation through Jesus Christ, it could be pointing to the openness of those middle class to accepting Jesus as the way of salvation.

The Challenge of the Gospel for the Middle Class

The contemporary middle class are a class with a new identity. They are also struggling with the tension between the cherished traditional religious and social values (including caste) which many are not willing to give up and the new opportunities for wealth and prosperity. It may not be an exaggeration if we say that there is a great amount of confusion of the real nature of God and religion.

If the Christian gospel is calling people to "sell everything that you have and come and follow me" it is something that will be very unacceptable for most of the middle class. The unexpected and abundant opportunity to become rich and enjoy the wealth and products is something that has come handy for them rather as a surprise. To give up all of that will be naturally too much to ask for. One possible way to respond to this situation is the proliferation of prosperity theology, where the desire for wealth and comforts go together with the presence of God. The alternative is an instruction that undermines the value of the material world and projects eternity and the world to come as more desirable.

By human reasoning the latter would be more acceptable to the poor and the deprived. Thus, the gospel was more appealing to those who are poor and deprived. The contemporary middle class are those who have tasted the world that is promised with prosperity and comforts. To tell them to give it all up would not be a welcome suggestion. Many of the middle class would have no other response to this invitation of the gospel than to "go away sad, because he was rich." The conclusion of the missionary in this case would be that "it is easier for a camel to pass through the eye of a needle than for the rich man to enter into the Kingdom of Heaven". But that is not the end of the story, but to know and believe that "what is impossible with man is possible with God."

Thus, while the Christian gospel has an inherent appeal to the poor and the deprived, there is also an evident possibility that the rich or newly rich middle class can be attracted to the gospel by the interference of God. We can see that while it was the poor and the deprived who constantly followed Jesus during his lifetime, there was another group of rich who followed him and were keen for what he was offering to them. Just as the question that the rich young ruler raised with Jesus was nothing of this earth but was keen to know how to receive eternal life. Yet, his wealth was the greatest obstacle to him. It is also to be noted that many of the poor who followed Jesus followed Him not because they "saw the miracles?" but because they "ate the bread." So those who would be stable disciples of Jesus are those who have concluded that eternal life is much more to be cherished than the material world.

A Strategy for Reaching the Middle Class

What could be a strategy to reach the urban and contemporary middle class? First, it has to do with the message. The message of the gospel must be communicated with conviction that eternity is of greater value than the earthly prosperity. Priority of eternity over the temporal does not mean that the person should turn ascetic or renounce basic comforts. However, there is a shift in priority. Along with that there should be a curb on greed. This teaching should also emphasize greater responsibility with our material possessions and help them to share. Teaching strongly on these may turn many away. However, this will also help many to resolve the conflict between the spiritual values and the material wealth that is already part of their struggle. Another element of teaching that will be of great importance to reaching the middle class is the teaching about God and his person. As we see from the Interserve survey, one of the major areas of conflict for the middle class (we do not know if this is true for the other classes in the society too) is about relating with God. 81% of those surveyed agreed that they pray at least one time a day. But there is much difference on what they understand prayer to be.

Secondly, it is important to use the method that are commonly used by the middle class to communicate among themselves. Varma repeatedly emphasize that one of the factors that unite the middle class of today is the connectivity, including Television and the social media. Use of social media and internet for reaching the middle class is important as a medium through which they can be reached. Churches and mission organizations should consider using the internet as a medium for the spread of the gospel. While there are special groups that are using the internet to spread the Christian gospel, it is also important to connect the 'virtual message' to real people. Therefore, Churches and organizations that are involved in interacting with people should use the internet for greater reach and teaching of the Christian truth. The existing organizations can use the already available resources on the net and promote those which they find most useful and monitor the people. The virtual world should also find ways of connecting with actual people.

An important step to reach the middle class is to reach them in the context of the social identity that they keep. It may not be entirely right to say that there is no focus on the middle class today. While it is true that there are not many ministries that concentrate on middle class per se, several ministries on professional and educational groups existing today are essentially focusing on the middle class. Ministries such as those among professionals, (Evangelical Medical Fellowship, Evangelical Graduates Fellowship, and many other similar organizations) are making an impact among the select professional groups. These professional groups have their access to many seekers as a result of the identity they can provide to others in the same category.

Promotion of literature that will to address the middle class challenge is also important. Missions and organizations that are involved in mission among middle class should be able to promote such literature.

The middle class is becoming more prominent and larger in number too, in the Indian community. The middle class is driven by the urge to succeed, become rich and spend. In the process they struggle with the tension between religious values and their material goals. The middle class has developed a pan Indian identity with the social connectivity that is very much part of their work and life. This identity is also a context in which they mutually share and impart a set of common values and goals. It is a challenge for the Church to present the gospel meaningfully to the middle class young of today, as there is apparent conflict of values between the gospel of Jesus and the aspirations of the contemporary middle class youth. At the same time there are traditional values and spiritual search that is present among the middle class. It is high time the

Church and mission organizations take up the goal of reaching the middle class making use of the connectivity of the group and addressing the spiritual and moral struggle that they are going through.

Endnotes

* **Dr John M Prasad** is an ordained minister in the St Thomas Evangelical Church of India and served until recently as the Principal of Jubilee Memorial Bible College, Chennai.

[1] Rukmini Srinivasan, "India Has No Middle Class," *Times of India*, May 6, 2010, accessed on January 16, 2012, http://articles.timesofindia.indiatimes.com/2010-05-06/india/28279518_1_middle-class-countries-definition.

[2] Srinivasan, "India Has No Middle Class."

[3] Pavan K. Varma, *The Great Indian Middle Class* (New Delhi: Penguin Books, 2007).

[4] Varma, *The Great Indian Middle Class*, xvii.

[5] Varma, *The Great Indian Middle Class*, xvii-xviii.

[6] The purchasing power of the contemporary middle class in India is attracting the attention of global business and they see the middle class in India as a big consumer market within the next few decades. The McKinsey report is basically an eye opener for the global business into the marketing opportunities among the middle class in India.

[7] The increasing number of farmer and student suicides resulting from efforts to climb up the ladder is indicative of this. The students who fail to make it to their ambition and the farmer who took loans hoping for a rich harvest and becomes a debtor instead are the typical categories of the suicide attempts.

[8] Varma, *The Great Indian Middle Class*, 46 & 47.

Bibliography

Srinivasan, Rukmini. "India Has No Middle Class." *Times of India*. May 6, 2010. http://articles.timesofindia.indiatimes.com/2010-05-06/india/28279518_1_middle-class-countries-definition

Varma, Pavan K. *The Great Indian Middle Class.* New Delhi: Penguin Books, 2007.

CHAPTER - 4

TEE Helps to Enable Christian Engagement with the Indian Middle Classes

*Eric Clouston**

Introduction

The Indian middle classes are expected to grow rapidly in the coming decades. Indeed, after significant growth for more than a decade, they have already emerged as a significant group both within the nation and within the Christian community. But Christian mission in India has traditionally focused on the underprivileged, so we now need to question whether our existing mission approaches and structures are suited to this rapidly changing environment. And this is a question with far-reaching implications. If we accept Bosch's assertion that, "The Christian faith… is intrinsically missionary"[2], then 'mission' is not a separate activity from 'church'. So, this question may have implications for any aspect of our Christian life and witness.

The emergence of increasing numbers of Indians who can be regarded as 'middle class' is already creating new opportunities for mission and ministry. There are increasing numbers of 'Middle class' Christians, whose networks of relationships and interactions, through work and leisure, bring them into regular contact with a wide range of other middle class Indians. I have the chance to observe this, living in Bangalore, the city which has led the way in India's involvement in the IT (Information Technology) and BPO (Business Process Outsourcing) sectors. There is, here, a new generation of relatively well-paid, cosmopolitan, ambitious, young workers who have much in common with the colleagues and clients I spent time with when I worked in the UK, for many years, in the technology sector, as a management consultant. Christians in such an environment, despite wanting to be good witnesses, may well feel daunted and many do not feel well-equipped.

Christians who want to get involved in mission and ministry have traditionally wanted to train at a residential college. But many cannot afford the fees or cannot afford to take several years away from their family or work commitments. So, TEE (Theological Education by Extension) emerged as a worldwide movement in the 1970's, allowing students to study part-time, in their home-place, by meeting in a small group with a local group-leader. In India, TAFTEE (The Association for Theological Education by Extension) was formed in 1971 and quickly proved itself effective, especially in training those involved in mission and ministry among the underprivileged. Naturally, many of those trained, especially at degree level and above, have always been from among the middle classes. In the past, their ministry was most often among the underprivileged. But increasing numbers of TAFTEE's students and graduates are now involved in mission and ministry among the middle classes, in a wide variety of ways.

This paper will start by discussing the emergence of the Indian middle classes, taking from published surveys and literature some key trends which are relevant to Christian mission. It will then mention some relevant examples of Christian engagement, taken from interviews with TAFTEE students. By reflecting on these examples and considering how they fit with the wider needs and opportunities, wider conclusions are then drawn about how the Church in India may need to respond in the years ahead.

The emergence of middle classes means that increasing numbers of Indians will find our traditional methods of mission irrelevant to their needs and interests. But it is also clear that there are already new, and different, opportunities for outreach among them. One suitable response will be for Indian churches to actively encourage and empower Christians for mission and ministry 'in the marketplace'. This will involve training a wide range of people – not just those in paid Christian work – and collaborating with them in this ministry. TEE is one suitable method for providing this training and for building supportive local groups.

What Do We Know About
the Emerging Indian Middle Class?

'Middle class' can be used to describe people with levels of family income. McKinsey use such a definition in their report "The 'Bird of Gold': The Rise of India's Consumer Market". For them, 'middle class' means people with "real annual disposable household incomes" of Rs 2,00,000 to 10,00,000.[3] On this basis, in 2005, the middle classes were about 5% of the population; and the report expects this to grow to 20% by 2015 and to 41% by 2025. The presence of these Middle classes is particularly noticeable in Bangalore, which has more than its 'fair share' of them. The signs include increasing numbers of private vehicles on the roads (although traffic congestion may now be limiting that); prominent advertising hoardings; shopping malls, often displaying western-style clothing; and increasing cost of living, with soaring prices of flats and land. India has long experienced a brain-drain of talented and ambitious youngsters emigrating, especially to the USA. But now, particularly since the US economy slowed in 2008/9, significant numbers who expected to remain overseas have begun returning to jobs here (certainly to Bangalore). Their earnings would be at the top end of 'middle class', or even higher. But, by contributing to the Indian economy, they can be expected to play a part in raising the earnings of many others.

But it is not necessary to assume a merely economic definition of 'middle class'. The term can alternatively be used to describe particular attitudes or behaviours (such as dress codes) associated with a middle class community. So, the significance will vary from country to country, and will evolve in time. The term can have meaning where there is an identifiable, established middle class. So, where there is relative stability, some consensus might emerge about what 'middle class attitudes' are. But in India, where this group is 'emerging' very rapidly, we should beware of assuming this. Here, most of the middle class were not born within that group, but entered it later, due to their family prospering. So, in India, we might be better to talk of 'the middle classes', because this includes a wide range of groups with very different backgrounds and identities; and there is a rapid pace of change, as new groups join.

The difficulty of characterising the Middle classes can be illustrated by recent reports of their attitudes to corruption. One journalist and author claims that, "What explains the unending movement against bribery is an increasingly self-assured and impatient new middle class, which has finally attained self-respect and dignity and is being taken seriously by the media… (and) will no longer allow itself to be humiliated by public officials."[4] But another journalist complains that, "Middle-class people find it easier to bribe rather than going through the hassle of waiting for a long time to get their work done"[5]. This is one example of what Raghunathan criticises as the wider Indian tendency to behaviour involving 'defecting', for short-term personal gain, instead of 'cooperating' for the wider good[6]. Altruistic and improving society, or materialistic and self-centred? The Indian Middle classes should not be imagined as a homogeneous or consistent group!

'Middle class' is not how people tend to describe or introduce themselves – in any country, and certainly not in India, where mother-tongue, religion, home-place and caste may all be more significant in terms of identity. So, the term should be used with care when talking to somebody about their own identity - some might be confused, or even offended by the term!

Despite the complexity of characterising this diverse group, the McKinsey report does indicate some trends which are strongly associated with being 'Middle Class' in India. They include: more urban than rural (with ongoing migration to cities); increasing spending, particularly on communications (the top sector for growth), then health care, and then education.

The report comments: "Many consumers will engage in "choice-driven" consumption for the first time. …their patterns and tastes are not yet established and they have few brand loyalties."[7]

This is indeed an opportunity for entrepreneurial companies. But the issues are not the same for those offering their services in what we might call 'the religion industry'. For here there are very strong and established 'brand loyalties'!

This path of increasing prosperity depends, according to the report, on whether the government continues to pursue liberal economic policies. But others suggest a wider variety of uncertainties. For instance, Kancha Ilaiah controversially goes so far as to see India as "on the course for a civil war"[8], because, "The Brahman thinkers kept India a very backward nation and innovative thought was never allowed to develop"[9] so that, "The movement of India into the post-Hindu phase alone can release the forces of production..."[10]. He advocates widespread learning of English, on the basis that this has already helped to unite and liberate some underprivileged communities. Others would point to India's economic growth in the last decade, as evidence that Ilaiah's case against Hinduism is greatly overstated. Nevertheless, his views do serve as a reminder that, whether on social or perhaps on environmental grounds, it is far from certain that the current growth in prosperity is truly sustainable.

Interserve's 2011 survey of the attitudes of middle class Indians shifts the emphasis from their spending to their spirituality. The results would be more revealing if broken down according to religion (respondents were 71% Hindu, 12% Moslem, 9% Buddhist, 8% other; but initial results are presented with all these grouped together). If it were possible to obtain responses also from poorer Indians, that would make it easier to demonstrate what is different about these wealthier respondents. But the survey does give some helpful indications:

– Faith remains strong. Despite Ilaiah's aspiration for an abandonment of Hinduism, most respondents remain both nominally a member of a religion (97% from the main Indian religions) and claiming to believe (only 4% say there is 'no God', another 4% see God as 'illusion'). Only 15% don't pray. So, any apologetics aimed at agnostics or atheists remains largely irrelevant.

– Reservations about religion. 38% were prepared to call religion 'human-made', which suggests some reservations or even suspicion. So effective witness will surely require evidence of genuineness.

– Boundaries are blurred. These are nominally non-Christians, yet 9% accept that forgiveness is available through Christ and a surprising 29% accept that he is the only way of salvation. Perhaps they are trying to please the questioner with an acceptable answer. More likely, they are happy to combine a mixture of beliefs.

– They may not be only materialistic. Only 10% selected 'richness' as what they most need in life, with many more (47%) selecting 'peace of mind'. Although they are prosperous, and our media culture seems increasingly materialistic, this wording suggests that they may not be merely materialistic in their concerns.

– They may need friends more than they admit. In 'responding to life's challenges', 59% said that their reaction is to 'work hard', and it is sad to note that only 16% would 'share with friends'. It seems that the culture, perhaps especially in the workplace, is not to appear weak, but simply to cope. Yet, in the face of struggles, whether or not support is expected or asked for, there may be a real opportunity for friends to help.

— Most have heard about Jesus. 72% say they have heard about Jesus 'many times' – although we do not know whether this is from Christians, or simply what other non-Christians say about Jesus. So, most respondents will have pre-conceived ideas about Jesus and Christians will have to spend time listening carefully to understand these.

— There is openness to Christians. It is encouraging that 58% were prepared to describe a Christian as 'good friend', with only 19% choosing 'no relationship' (the most negative response available). This suggests that the opportunity is there, for building friendships as a starting point for outreach.

The survey responses suggest an encouraging level of friendliness and openness to engage with Christians and with their message, even though nearly half believe that your religion is determined by your birth. And, even though opposition to conversion has been so vocal in India, this group was surprisingly open – they are almost evenly divided on the question of whether one should change religion. But we should note that, if one of them were to become a Christian, the attitude of their parents would also matter – and they are likely to be dispossessed and excluded from the family.

In summary, the Indian middle classes include people with a wide range of different backgrounds and identities, who may have little in common other than their increasing prosperity. But there are some clear trends. These include: urbanization, including migration to the cities; increasing literacy in the major languages, especially English; access to communications (TV, mobile phones, internet and all the content that goes with them); access to healthcare; concern for education (and thus, especially for the next generation, increasing levels of education). These changes do not seem to have led any significant proportion to abandon their faith or religious identity. But there seem to be higher levels of open-mindedness, awareness of other ideas and beliefs and perhaps more opportunity and willingness to question and discuss.

How Does Existing Christian Mission Relate to the Middle Classes?

A recent summary of cross-cultural mission in India classified the five main types of mission here as: "evangelism... church planting among people groups... translation ministry... social concern ministry... children and youth ministry" (e.g. through VBS, Vacation Bible Schools)[11]. Under these headings, we can see how these traditional forms of Christian mission, while remaining relevant for most of the Indian population, will have decreasing relevance or effectiveness among the emerging middle classes.

'Evangelism' is, of course, relevant to all. But the ministry of 'evangelism' is currently mainly carried out by professional evangelists, funded by gifts from Christians who support their ministry. This approach to evangelism, if used among the Middle classes, will cost more, because it involves living in more expensive locations and requires evangelists who are themselves more Middle class – following the 'Homogeneous Unit Principle' that evangelistic communication is most effective between people who are similar. And it may be harder to persuade donors to support work among those who are already relatively privileged. A survey of south Indian mission agencies has also shown that it is increasingly difficult to recruit suitable evangelists:

> Not many young people are motivated for missions, the primary reasons being the lack of glamour in such a calling and the minimal financial compensation packages. The era of sacrificial living is almost lost, with the new generation presently refusing to shoulder this task.[12]

'Church-planting among people groups' has been effective among clearly-identifiable groups, such as particular 'scheduled tribe' groups or 'scheduled caste' groups. For example, FMPB's work among the Malto tribe has been so successful that TAFTEE's training materials are now being translated into the Malto language so that indigenous church leaders can be trained. However, the Middle classes are not homogeneous enough to be described as a 'people group'. That would imply an existing, stable culture, social structure and network of relationships. Church-planting among the Middle classes is certainly needed and happening. But their networks of relationships are very different, and more fluid, so the approach to outreach and the structure of resulting churches need to be rather different.

'Translation ministry' is less significant for the Middle classes, because more of them are fluent in the main Indian languages, where Bibles and other materials already exist. And many use English, or at least aspire to.

'Social concern ministry' is most important for the underprivileged. The Middle Classes have less need: of mission hospitals, or of 'healing rallies', because they can afford increasing levels of health care; of AIDS programmes, as they are the ones increasingly aware of how to avoid infection; of orphanages, as they have less difficulty affording to raise their own children (and can afford abortions, if necessary).

'Children and youth ministry' is needed by all; but Middle Class children are less likely to be attracted to VBS or similar events, because they have an increasing range of other options for entertainment, and may also have increasing pressure from parents to attend extra academic, musical or sporting classes.

In all of these areas, the middle classes are moving on, and no longer 'fit' with our traditional approaches to mission. So, what changes in approach may be needed, if our evangelism, church-planting and youth ministry are to 'fit' with them?

Mission Tailored for the Middle Classes

There have, historically, been mission efforts targeted at particular 'class' groups. Roland Allen (writing in 1912) mentions "a striking example of the wonderful results which may be obtained by a judicious appeal to an influential class... the 'Natural Foot Society' in China... (which) began by enlisting the support of enlightened and well-to-do official and commercial families."[13] But he goes on to suggest that this was not St Paul's approach; rather, that Paul went to key centres (cities) and preached to whoever would listen – relying less on strategy than on taking opportunities under the guidance of the Holy Spirit[14]. Similarly, Green concludes that, "The spread of early Christianity was... largely accomplished by informal missionaries and must have been to a large extent haphazard and spontaneous."[15] So mission with a rigid strategy of focusing only on the Middle Classes would be inappropriate, if that meant a neglect of mission among others, such as the underprivileged. Programmes with these different focuses should ideally happen alongside each other, not as alternatives or in competition – because they are each only part of the overall *missio Dei*, which is "greater than the observable missionary enterprise."[16]

There is growing interest in evangelism carried out by Christians, not for pay but in the course of their 'normal' lives. Among the Middle Classes, this may be more appropriate than sending paid evangelists, for reasons discussed above. This approach was one focus of the 'decade of evangelism' proclaimed by the Church of England for the 1990's. And it is happening in Asia. Chang mentions various approaches: "Marketplace Ministry" (outreach through the normal, public relationships of work and everyday life); "Tentmaking" (working to earn a living, in order to have opportunities for outreach in any free time); and "Business as Mission" (creating a business with the aims of both profit and godly witness e.g. aiming to contribute to social transformation)[17]. Chang makes the case that that, despite prevailing prejudice among Christians,

> ...business people are *not* second-class citizens in God's kingdom. In fact, they are probably in the most strategic position to reach people in the marketplace who, under normal circumstances, have little or no opportunity to be in contact with a pastor or missionary or to hear the good news.[18]

Although not listed above, the church itself is "essentially missionary"[19]. So, Church life can be an opportunity for outreach[20] – normally, to people of similar background to those within the church. But the trends we have considered above mean that people of different backgrounds may, gradually, have more in common as they become middle class. And migration to the cities means that urban churches can increasingly get involved in cross-cultural mission in their own area. So, there are increasing opportunities, for churches which have some middle class members, to reach out to middle class non-Christians around them, even if their background is very different. But there is a question about what style of church they will be able to relate to. A church which teaches only dogmatically, with no opportunity for questioning or discussion, will be hard for a non-Christian to engage with. A church which focuses strongly on representing people with a cultural identity – be that Dalit, Anglo-Indian or whatever – will, of course, struggle to make others feel that they can belong. But urban churches, certainly in Bangalore, have increasing opportunities to attract a range of people and are facing up to the challenges of catering for multiple languages.

So, there are opportunities for churches to develop their own outreach by deliberately adapting their approach and style to make it easy for outsiders to get involved. Rick Warren has been influential in advocating this[21]. But his approach (he founded a new church, Saddleback, California, 'from scratch') does little to consider the complexities of trying to address the needs of both an existing congregation and of these interested outsiders. In practice, in many churches, in India and elsewhere, it is more practical to plant a new church with a different emphasis (outreach-focused). So there may be a need to plant churches which are designed especially to reach out to 'Middle Class' Indians.

Examples of How TEE Students have been Involved
TAFTEE has students all over India (and some in other countries). Rather less than half are pastors, with others having a wide variety of backgrounds, employment and ministry involvement. Some of our courses are at degree- and postgraduate-level and, for these, our tutors and students are, of course, well-educated and can be described as 'middle class'. And, especially in the cities, there are significant numbers whose ministries are primarily among the middle classes. For example, of a batch who completed post-graduate studies

(MTh) recently, a quarter (5 out of 20) were already involved in ministries which fall clearly into this sector.

Here are ten examples, arising from interviews since 2010:

— A highly qualified researcher, in a government technology organisation, had a Hindu village background, and then his family became Christians when he was a teenager. At work, he has arranged for a group of his colleagues to get together to study TAFTEE's degree course. This has helped to equip them to be godly witnesses, especially in their workplace. Over the years, the group has grown to about a dozen.

— A TAFTEE student in Bangalore noticed the needs of the workers involved in the city's massive IT industry and call-centres – mainly young and educated, but often working antisocial shift patterns and away from family, having come to the city especially for work. In 2005, he started a Christian fellowship catering especially to their needs e.g. by having meetings at flexible times during the week, rather than fixed Sunday services. This work has been growing by planting house churches, and by training others in church planting (including training delivered on radio).

— An executive of a large, national insurance company handles, as well as her technical work, classes on management topics that include Leadership Skills, Communication Skills, Team Management, Time Management, and Stress Busting – a real opportunity to influence colleagues. As well as studying with TAFTEE, she has also been organising and teaching TAFTEE groups and also providing regular counselling for missionaries with an Indian mission organisation.

— With an MBA, long experience in the world of Projects in the IT industry, and a particular interest in the dynamics of Indian business, one TAFTEE graduate now runs interactive workshops and seminars which aim to 'challenge and equip Christian Business owners and professionals to transform the marketplace toward the Kingdom'.

— A TAFTEE graduate in Bangalore found that his studies helped him develop in his role as a leader in a Christian organisation reaching out to young people, especially college students. His role, which initially had a local focus, now includes international responsibilities, with similar campus work going on in various Asian countries.

— One entrepreneur, after completing a TAFTEE degree, started a group of companies dealing with microfinance and building social housing (now also beginning to build schools and hospitals). Alongside this, he has started a "School of Christian Leadership and Management", providing a 3-year degree in English, plus a broad training in Christian leadership and mission, including such courses as investigative journalism and mass communication. The courses involve exposure, not only to the traditional 'mission' sector, but also to the NGO sector, the corporate sector and social enterprises.

— One ambitious young IT worker heard God's call through outreach meetings held at the YMCA where he was staying. A few years later, he feels that his calling is to strengthen others in their faith, particularly through the visual media. In collaboration with others, he has produced a DVD of the book of James, re-told in a modern Indian context, initially in English and Tamil. They also provide a leaflet of questions which arise from the DVD, to help to encourage discussion.

– A professor in a secular university, who previously taught for a Christian organisation for a few years, now runs TAFTEE courses in his spare time. This is both for groups through his local church and for groups of local students, from his college and from other local colleges. Most are of Christian background, but not all. One, from a non-Christian background, completed the course and has now herself started teaching a group in her own village.

– One of our students in Hyderabad, a pastor with a background directing youth work, has now planted an English-language church among the young professionals there, who originate from other parts of India. Most are under the age of 30. They are now involved in planting similar churches in other locations. Previous generations may have looked for leaders who were simply charismatic, but he feels that young professionals now need and are looking for leaders with a depth of wisdom, which has made his TEE training especially helpful.

These examples demonstrate a wide variety of ministries. Only one (the last) is a conventional, full-time pastor – and he has an unconventional form of church, because they deliberately focus on engaging with young professionals. And one other (involved in youth and campus outreach) is a full-time Christian worker. The others are all professionals or entrepreneurs who want to use their technical or business skills to create opportunities for ministry among the Middle Classes – be that students, those in business, professionals, or just people who are willing to watch a Bible-based DVD and discuss it. These ministries do not fit one, standard approach. Rather, they are each tailored, arising from the opportunities and abilities of that mission-minded Christian.

The abilities, motivation and achievements of these Christians are impressive, and may seem rather daunting. Some of them had a relatively privileged start in life; others have had to 'work their way up'. But they are all exceptional – not only because of their particular ministries (which is why they were chosen for mention here), but also because they have managed to train in theology, part-time, at degree-level or higher. That is how I had opportunity to interview them.

So, what can we learn from their examples? Are their ministries unique and unrepeatable, or can others hope in some way to follow their example?

Conclusions for Future Engagement with the Emerging Indian Middle Classes

The rapid emergence of middle classes does not in any way invalidate existing Christian mission among the poor and underprivileged. We must not neglect this, perhaps tougher and more strenuous ministry, which is still desperately needed – and will be for the foreseeable future. But it will be not a bad thing, if some long-term missions find that their community prospers over the years, so that their work simply evolves into a ministry among the middle class.

Some well-established forms of mission will become increasingly relevant – for instance, campus ministry, as numbers of students increase; and hospital chaplaincy, as demand for healthcare increases.

But the ministries of our TEE students suggest that the key new opportunity for mission and ministry among the middle classes comes through the natural contacts which become more possible with increasing communications and networking. The barriers or hurdles between a non-Christian and a Christian become lower, and the opportunities increase for contact, dialogue, friendship and influence, as both become more 'middle class'. Valuable help may no longer be necessities, but coaching in English, counselling, mentoring, making helpful introductions, computer advice, etc.

So, it is 'normal' Christians, rather than those in full-time ministry, who are in the front-line of this mission. And it is challenging. With improved access to healthcare, healings (whether medical or miraculous) become less significant. As people become more educated, claims of authority (whether my authority to speak for God, or the Bible's) become less credible. There is more need to be able to discuss and persuade – not only by words, but also by attitudes and behaviour which demonstrate the truth and genuineness of what we say.

To be involved in this, it helps to be part of a local church which sees such outreach as a natural part of its own mission and will therefore encourage and support – and actively welcome any non-Christians who come to find out more. Such a church must be prepared for the fact that, if outreach is successful, interested non-Christians may keep attending. And, if new people become members, the church will change. Middle class newcomers may be people of great ability, and a church has to be willing to help them, not only to belong, but also to develop and use their gifts.

Our students affirm that their TEE training has been truly helpful to their ministries – giving them 'tools' they need to meet these challenges. TEE involves studying in local groups, which provides not only the opportunity to learn from each other, but also the opportunity to support, encourage and pray for each other. Other forms of training, shorter than a degree course, may be more appropriate for many. TAFTEE offers a course on 'Discipleship and Ministry' which can be completed in less than 2 years. As mentioned above, workshops and seminars are also available – an approach which the Haggai Institute has been using to provide Christian leadership training, internationally since 1969 and in India since 1988.

As India becomes more prosperous, we can expect increasing competition between the various 'brands' of the religion industry – clamouring for people's allegiance and for their Rupees! As people become better informed they may also become more cynical. But Christians they meet can bring Good News which, through all the noise, will ring true if we speak it and live it faithfully. Christians need to be trained and supported in our role as Christ's ambassadors here.

Endnotes

* **Dr. Eric Clouston** is Education Consultant, attached to TAFTEE (The Association for Theological Education by Extension), Bangalore, since 2009 and sent as a Mission Partner by CMS (Church Mission Society), UK.

[1] David J. Bosch, *Transforming Mission: Paradigm Shifts in the Theology of Mission* (Maryknoll: Orbis Books, 1991), 8.

[2] Jonahan Ablet, *et al.*, *The 'Bird of Gold': The Rise of India's Consumer Market* (McKinsey Global Institute, May 2007), 11, accessed on January 4, 2012, https://www.mckinsey.com/featured-insights/asia-pacific/the-bird-of-gold.

[3] Gurcharan Das, "Middle Class Gets Back Its Dignity," *Times of India Blogs*, July 10, 2011, accessed January 4, 2012, http://blogs.timesofindia.indiatimes.com/men-and-ideas/entry/middle-class-gets-back-its-dignity.

[4] Sanchari Bhattacharya, "Middle-class Indians Find it Easier to Bribe," December 27, 2011, accessed January 4, 2012, http://www.rediff.com/news/slide-show/slide-show-1-corruption-middle-class-indians-find-it-easier-to-bribe/20111227.htm.

[5] V. Raghunathan, *Games Indians Play: Why We Are the Way We Are* (New Delhi: Penguin Books, 2006), 47.

[6] Ablet, *et al.*, *The 'Bird of* Gold', 105.

[7] Kancha Ilaiah, *Post-Hindu India: A Discourse in Dalit-Bahujan, Socio-Spiritual and Scientific Revolution* (New Delhi: Sage Publications, 2009), ix.

[8] Ilaiah, *Post-Hindu India*, 266.

[9] Ilaiah, *Post-Hindu India*, 295.

[10] Dino L. Touthang, "Cross-cultural Mission Movements in India," in *Emerging Mission Movements: Voices of Asia*, ed. Bambang Budijanto, 85-100, (Colorado Springs: Compassion International and Asia Evangelical Alliance, 2011), 89 - 91.

[11] Touthang, "Cross-cultural Mission Movements in India," 99.

[12] Roland Allen, *Missionary Methods: St Paul's or Ours?* (Grand Rapids: Eerdmans, 1962), 18.

[13] Allen, *Missionary Methods*, 16 & 19.

[14] Michael Green, *Evangelism in the Early Church* (Eastbourne: Kingsway, 2003), 356.

[15] Bosch, *Transforming Mission*, 519.

[16] Philip Chang, "Business as Mission in Asia," in *Emerging Mission Movements: Voices of Asia*, ed. Bambang Budijanto, 11-22, (Colorado Springs: Compassion International and Asia Evangelical Alliance, 2011), 12.

[17] Chang, "Business as Mission in Asia," 15.

[18] Bosch, *Transforming Mission*, 372.

[19] C. Van Engen, *God's Missionary People: Rethinking the Purpose of the Local Church* (Grand Rapids: Baker Books, 1991).

[20] Rick Warren, *The Purpose Driven Church* (Grand Rapids: Zondervan, 1995).

Bibliography

Ablet, Jonahan Aadarsh Baijal, Eic Beinhocker, Anupam Bose, Diana Farrel, Ulrich Gersch, Ezra Greenberg, Shishir Gupta, and Sumit Gupta. *The 'Bird of Gold': The Rise of India's Consumer Market.* McKinsey Global Institute, May 2007. https://www.mckinsey.com/featured-insights/asia-pacific/the-bird-of-gold.

Allen, Roland. *Missionary Methods: St Paul's or Ours?* Grand Rapids: Eerdmans, 1962.

Bhattacharya, Sanchari. "Middle-class Indians Find it Easier to Bribe." December 27, 2011. http://www.rediff.com/news/slide-show/slide-show-1-corruption-middle-class-indians-find-it-easier-to-bribe/20111227.htm.

Bosch, David J. *Transforming Mission: Paradigm Shifts in the Theology of Mission.* Maryknoll: Orbis Books, 1991.

Chang, Philip. "Business as Mission in Asia." In *Emerging Mission Movements: Voices of Asia.* Edited by Bambang Budijanto,11-22. Colorado Springs: Compassion International and Asia Evangelical Alliance, 2011.

Das, Gurcharan. "Middle Class Gets Back Its Dignity." *Times of India Blogs* July 10, 2011. http://blogs.timesofindia.indiatimes.com/men-and-ideas/entry/middle-class-gets-back-its-dignity.

Engen, C. Van. *God's Missionary People: Rethinking the Purpose of the Local Church.* Grand Rapids: Baker Books, 1991.

Green, Michael. *Evangelism in the Early Church.* Eastbourne: Kingsway, 2003.

Ilaiah, Kancha. *Post-Hindu India: A Discourse in Dalit-Bahujan, Socio-Spiritual and Scientific Revolution.* New Delhi: Sage Publications, 2009.

Raghunathan, V. *Games Indians Play: Why We are the Way We are.* New Delhi: Penguin Books, 2006.

Touthang, Dino L. "Cross-cultural Mission Movements in India." In *Emerging Mission Movements: Voices of Asia.* Edited by Bambang Budijanto, 85-100. Colorado Springs: Compassion International and Asia Evangelical Alliance, 2011.

Warren, Rick. *The Purpose Driven Church.* Grand Rapids: Zondervan, 1995.

CHAPTER - 5

An Interview with a Member of US Middle Class and Possible Implication for Ministry

Vicki Brown *

Introduction

In the edited text by Amita Baviskar and Raka Ray (2011), *Elite and Everyman; The Cultural Politics of the Indian Middle Classes,* there are two chapters that this essay will use as a background to talking about the middle class in the United States. In particular, the chapter by Seemin Qayum and Raka Ray, *The Middle Class at Home*, inspired the relating of the following information in narrative form. Qayum and Ray's research involved two generations of Bengali middle class, 80 in-depth interviews, and a survey of 500 middle-class households.

Since 'distinction' is the basis of class formation, Qayum and Ray's argument is "classes come into being not only through production and consumption…outside the household, but through labour and *intimate practices within the home*"[1] (emphasis added), particularly in a society with a long history of domestic servitude, such as India. Though there are considerable cultural differences between US and Indian practices in regard to just the keeping of domestic help, I feel there are still some commonalities that making a comparison might be justified in the effort to describe the middle class in the US. I will embed some socio/cultural information within the narrative of an interview of one US family, as well as suggest one possible means of ministering to the Indian middle class.

The White Family

The study of the home is justified because it is there that class distinctions are consciously and unconsciously portrayed and reproduced. When we talk about 'class', we are talking about social stratification—ways in which a society elevates certain categories of people, giving some more wealth, power, and prestige than others. All human societies are stratified, that is, people within any society will be socially unequal. Class systems are based on both birth (caste elements) and individual achievement.

Information concerning the White family (a pseudonym) will cover three generations. Covering three generations will magnify the meaning of both *meritocracy* and *status consistency*. Defining classes in US is difficult because of our relatively low level of status consistency, that is, there is some chance of social mobility. Especially toward the middle of this hierarchy, people's standing in one of three dimensions (i.e., income, status or social prestige, and power) may not be the same as their standing in another. For example, many members of the clergy enjoy great prestige, but have moderate power and low pay. Finally, the social characteristic of class systems—again, in the US, most pronounced around the middle—means that social position may change during a person's lifetime, further blurring class boundaries.[2] The White family demonstrates how, in the US, status consistency can be low.

The status of the White family will be based on the present household status of the two senior married adults, Richard and Anna. The early social status of both sets of parents and grandparents of Richard and Anna range from what we, in the US, term as lower-class poor to working-class. Both sets of parents grew up during The Great Depression 1929 and subsequently grew up hard working and frugal. Anna's father, in particular, grew up in a poor, single mother environment and spent some time in a boy's home because of her grandmother's inability to support her offspring. Though Anna's mother grew up poor her family was land-owning farmers. Near the close of World War II the government paid Anna's mother's way to become a registered nurse. She was the only member of her family to finish a post high school education.

However, it is questionable whether Anna's father actually finished high school before joining the Marines as a cook at the beginning of WW II. After the war Anna's parents met and married while he was a floor attendant and she a floor charge nurse. Their living was frugal. But in the 1950's the post WW II economy was growing and so were opportunities. Anna's father gradually gained expertise in ultrasonic engineering and in the 1970's started his own company, partly financed by money borrowed from Anna's farming family. Some family members argue that the smartest thing Anna's father did was marry her mother—during the lean times she kept the family financially afloat by working as a nurse while raising a large family, but she also worked for Anna's father when she was home.

Anna's parents' hard work paid off; the company became more profitable and when Anna's father hired her husband,

Richard, it became more and more profitable and more complex. The company became so complex that at her father's death he no longer could explain most of the processes used to produce products for the new emerging market—computer hardware. Some in the family argue that the second smartest thing Anna's father did was hire her husband. Richard was the first in his family to graduate from college, but his degree was not in engineering, it was philosophy. But Richard was and is very intelligent and although his getting hired may smack at nepotism it was his hard work and intrepid research that brought the company into the 21st century. It was also Richard's personality.

Anna's father had the typical entrepreneurial personality—creative, energetic, and volatile—so volatile he was unable to keep his better workers. But Richard's personality was steady, tolerant, and diplomatic. Many entrepreneurial efforts have failed due to the inability of the founder to transition a company into more steady hands, but Anna's father was able to do it; no doubt in part because Richard was a member of the family.

Overview of US Class System

Sociologists divide the US class system a little differently, but the following is a customary division. At the very top is the *upper-upper class*, Karl Marx's capitalist—owners of the means of production or owners of most of the nation's private wealth. This group, referred to as "blue bloods", or "old money", comprise about 1 percent of the population. This group primarily inherit their wealth and historically this class has been composed mostly of white Anglo-Saxon Protestants.

Most upper-class people actually fall into the *lower-upper class*. The major difference between this group and the upper-

upper class is that the lower-upper class are the "working rich" who get their money mostly by earning it rather than through inheritance. This group comprises 3 to 4 percent of the US population.

The whole of US *middle-class* makes up 40 to 45 percent of the population. Our large middle-class contains far more racial and ethnic diversity than the upper-class. In this organizational scheme this class is made up of upper-middles and average middles. *The upper-middle class* have rewarding careers, such as physicians and business executives. They are able to live in comfortable homes, and build investments. Their children go to good schools and will usually graduate from college. This group often play an important role in local political affairs. *Average-middle class*, on the other hand, typically work at less prestigious white collar jobs such as bank managers, school teachers, or in highly skilled blue-collared jobs such as electrical work. This group are likely to be high school graduates but only about half will complete a college degree, usually at a less expensive school.[3]

The *working-class* (sometimes called lower-middle class) make up about 30 percent of the US population. They form, in Marxist terms, the core of the industrial proletariat, and usually work under constant supervision. Their blue-collar jobs prevent them from building little or no wealth. These jobs also offer fewer benefits, such as health insurance and pension plans, leaving them vulnerable to financial problems due to illness.[4]

The remaining 20 percent of the US population make up the lower-class. A subset of this group, the "working poor", fair slightly better, holding low-prestige, low-income jobs. Society segregates the lower class, especially when the poor are racial or ethnic minorities. Fewer than half own their homes, but these homes will typically be in the least desirable neighbourhoods. Barely half complete high school, and only one in four ever reaches college.[5]

To return to the White family a moment, it is necessary to describe here the nature of the White family's company lest one mistakenly assume this company was a large, billion-dollar, multinational corporation; it wasn't. The company was relatively small, nestled in a county of Ohio composed mostly of farmers. It was a modest sized company, about 250 employees, found in rural America. But, it had cornered a market niche in the computer industry that needed its specialized machining process that was necessary for the production of computers. In 2006 Richard sold the company to a large national computer company. Subsequently, Richard and Anna's income and wealth increased considerably. They became, objectively by income and wealth standards, lower-upper class. Though born into working-class families, they achieved in their adulthood lower-upper class, and became what is frequently referred to as the 'nouveau riche', or the new rich. But how should their new status/class be perceived and explained? The remainder of this essay will attempt to describe how the White family adapted to their new status, and with the theoretical aid of Max Weber and the erudite text by Baviskar and Ray, I will attempt to explain their status in light of modern rationality and ideology.

Max Weber and Dimensions of Inequality

There are a number of theories that address the rise of the modern system and social stratification, but the one that I favour is one developed by sociologist Max Weber (1864-1920). Weber's social analysis is multifaceted rather than attributing the modern industrial/ post-industrial phenomena to a single catalyst or attribute. As to the rise of modernity, Weber attributed its rise to a new way of thinking. *Rationality* is a way of thinking in a modern society that emphasizes deliberate, matter-of-fact calculation of the most efficient way to accomplish a particular task. A rational worldview is task oriented, whereas traditional worldview is relationship oriented.

While a class system may be a novel experience for Indians, the caste system is still felt. Caste is still mostly observed in rural areas, where agriculture demands a lifelong routine of hard physical work. But a caste system can exist only within a society bound by tradition, values and beliefs passed from generation to generation, effectively limiting personal choices. One of Weber's major contributions towards an understanding of the social stratification is the notion of *ideology*. Ideology is the basis that determines the type of society and the kind of stratification found in a given society, whether closed (caste) or open (class). The traditional worldview, a worldview that does not value change, underpins the caste system, a worldview that values social position as a moral responsibility. The ideology that undergirds the United States, however, is the concept of meritocracy.

Meritocracy refers to social stratification based on *personal* merit, which includes a person's acquired knowledge, abilities, and effort. Whereas a person from a traditional worldview has a 'collective' mindset, a person from a rational meritocracy has an 'individualistic' mindset. Meritocracy in industrial societies teaches people to expect unequal rewards based on *individual* performance; wealth and power are won by those individuals who perform the best. Further, this means that the poor come to be looked down on as *personally* undeserving. A capitalist society encourages one to think that way. Theoretically, in a pure form of meritocracy, it would follow that those who were the smartest and hardest working would reap the greatest rewards in a society, regardless their status at birth. Such a system would have ongoing social mobility (very low status consistency), blurring social categories as individuals continuously move up or down in the system, depending on their latest performance. But a pure meritocracy does not exist. In reality, a meritocracy contains caste elements for a couple of reasons. First, families and religion, two major realities for humans, cannot be evaluated on the basis of economic performance. Second, the ideology of meritocracy glosses over the caste elements of the very rich and very poor. It is known that one is 'born' into wealth just as one is 'born' into poverty. The family one is born into very much determines the life-chances and success that can be achieved as an individual. Class systems in industrial societies move toward meritocracy to promote productivity and efficiency, but need to keep some caste elements, such as family, to maintain order and social unity. But poverty, a very negative caste element, limits the choices of thousands of people in any society (and, adds insult-to-injury by making them feel guilty for it), and thereby, precludes the possibility of a pure meritocracy.

For a society to continue to be content with living in a meritocracy, a meritocracy must supply enough rags-to-riches stories in order to justify its ongoing existence. A chapter in the Baviskar and Ray text by Carol Upadhya, "Software and the 'New' Middle Class in the 'New India'" demonstrates how India's version of 'Horatio Alger' narratives legitimizes newly found wealth among Indian entrepreneurs. Apparently such one is a man by the name, Narayana Murthy. Murthy was born into poverty, in a "dusty village", one of eight children. Much is made of his early hardship before his Infosys Company went public. The narrative of his life not only emphasizes his personal ability and hard work, but his modest mode of living and his claim to being middle class. According to Upadhya, "his own narratives about his career and success extol 'traditional middle-class values' as a key to economic prosperity, and emphasize that the accumulation of wealth is not for personal gain but for the larger good of society…his symbolic power, I suggest, comes precisely from his successful retailing of a middle-class image, through which his personal fortune and elite status are successfully effaced."[6] Further, she states:

> …Murthy story appeals to the aspiring middle classes because it demonstrates that it is possible to be successful in business and accumulate wealth while retaining the cultural identity that gives the middle class its ideological power. Murthy embodies the 'old middle class' values of austerity, service to the nation and self-sacrifice, played out within the new ideology of the market. In these narratives, 'middle class' signifies not privilege and dominance but modest economic standing, hard work, and commitment to national-development goals…These narratives and media images are central to the construction of the dominant ideology of the new middle class and the *legitimization of its position*"[7] (emphasis added).

The White family's story is an echo of Murthy's story: One can acquire wealth without alienating one's community if one adheres to their middle class values. The White family maintains the good-will of their farming community by maintaining their middle class values of hard work despite an income that is over the middle-class limits. They accomplish this by living with relative modesty on a farm. They eschew most conspicuous consumption, such as large and costly vehicles and elaborate appliances. They continue to be active in their local church and are involved in various church based international humanitarian organizations. They maintain good relations with a wide range of social class members by hiring lower income individuals during this time of high unemployment rates; they attempt to find work for them to do on the farm despite this time of stock fragility, thereby putting their wealth at risk. They provide houses at very low rent for those unable to afford homes. They are involved in local projects that aid the handicapped in their community. In addition, after the sale of the company Richard could have retired, but instead started another company so as to provide continuing local employment for others. They do all this in part because they are Christians and care for the welfare of others, but also because they want to continue to be considered a part of their community rather than be considered trying to be "high-minded".

But one area of their lifestyle gives emphasis to their new class status and creates a divide between their lifestyle and that of most others in their community, and that is in the hiring of domestic help. At one given time, when they assumed the raising of two other children, they hired one nanny (full-time), two tutors, gardeners, a meal brought in once a week, and a housekeeper who cleaned twice a week. While hiring "cleaning ladies" is not unusual for households where both adults work, it is unusual for a household where the woman does not work outside the home, as is the case of the White's. The extent of household help as a distinguishing attribute of U.S lower-upper class also reveals to be a factor in identifying the culture of the middle class in India according to Qayum and Ray.

The Middle Classes at Home—In India

In their chapter, Qayum and Ray give findings of their study of middle class Bengali households, and argue that the manner of keeping domestic help serves to distinguish the old and the new middle class, and also, the keeping of domestic help a dominant attribute that identifies the culture of the Indian middle class as a whole. In their account they contrast the narrative content between the old traditional middle class and the new middle class. They found that the biggest differences between the two were the procurement of and keeping of servants. The old middle class, based on long tradition, still attempted to maintain live-in servants. These live-in servants are considered to be life-long relationships, with strong bonds loyalty and affection. Loyalty and mutual affection created life-long allegiances in the "big house" of the old middle class. The new middle class, on the other hand, still maintained servants, but because of space constraints hired outside help, usually part-time. The new middle class tended to hire on contractual basis, reflecting, according to Qayum and Ray, the new market mindset of the new Indian middle class. Whereas the old middle class enjoyed the loyalty and mutual affection of their servants, the relationship between the new middle class and their servants tended to be short-lived, and strained due to the smaller living quarters of the new middle class.[8]

Returning to the lifestyle of the US middle class—hired help usually do not live in the household, and are part-time. Having live-in, full-time servants would be an attribute of the upper-class where incomes and homes are considerably larger. Also, among US middle class, relationships between part-time help and employees are contractual and frequently tenuous, and in this they have more in common with the new Indian middle class. But the Whites diverge from what is common practice in regard to closeness of relationships, and relating how they may differ gets to the main purpose of this paper—that is, where might we find potential areas of ministry among both US and Indian middle class?

The White Family Revisited

Anna White related the following story to me. Only the nanny, who was full-time, and the gardeners, were contractual. The employment of the rest of the staff, namely tutors, house cleaner, and cook for one meal, were based on verbal agreements. All of these employees were Christians, some from other churches other than her own, and one from an old-order Christian background. Anna relates that at this time the household was full of emotional turmoil, between worries over one delinquent child and the stress of trying to help two children with various developmental disabilities. One day she was particularly distressed and was constantly on the verge of weeping. On this day, as she was distractedly walking down the hall, she was approached by the children's nanny. "She stopped me and looked at me deeply and then said, 'you need prayer.' She gathered all the others to me in the hall and as they laid hands on me they all took turns to pray for me. I can honestly say, that from that moment on things changed for the better. For one thing, I was better at coping. In my pain, I had emotionally isolated myself, but from these dear ladies I felt loved and affirmed." Anna further related that all these ladies still work for her and she considers them more friends than employees.

Based on my personal meditation on the above I would like to share some thoughts on not only how to reach India's middle class, but anyone from any culture, including my own. First, I have personally renewed my commitment to servanthood as portrayed by Christ, for surely this is a way of making Jesus visible. I need to examine and prayerfully work out being a servant among my family, friends, and acquaintances, but also become more aware of what being a servant looks like in my professional life. How can I be a servant to my colleagues? Can I esteem the thoughts and ways of my colleagues as higher than my own? Can I truly love a fellow teacher who may not be presenting himself as not very Christ-like at a particular moment; realizing that I, myself, also am far from obtaining the perfect mind of Christ?

And what does being a servant look like when working with students? Can I be understanding and compassionate without being a "push-over"? Can I teach future pastors and missionaries to not only be servants in their own lives, but also encourage them to teach their congregants that being a Christ-like servant is an important spiritual goal not only in their personal lives, but it is also an honourable goal as a vocation?

Based on Anna's experience I want to suggest that one way the Indian middle class can be reached with the love of Christ is through their domestic help. As domestic help they are privy to the needs of the home environment. No doubt the social divide between employer and help is culturally greater in the Indian home than in the US home, but the God of all will give guidance through his Spirit in how best and appropriately administer love in Jesus' name. How can we teach our future ministers and missionaries that we are all called to be servants of the Most High and any vocation that lends itself to service is a high-calling from God. Perhaps one way to explore possibilities of servanthood as an evangelistic tool is by developing a panel of teachers and students from several learning institutions. Afterwards, each group could convene together sometime later to consider outcomes of the discussions and ways to disseminate their findings. Paul's words help remind us:

Now I exhort you, brethren, by the name of our Lord Jesus Christ, that you all agree, and there be no divisions among you…but to those who are the called, both Jews and Greeks, Christ the power of God and the wisdom of God…God has chosen the foolish things of the world to shame the wise, and God has chosen the weak things of the world to shame the things which are strong, and the base things of the world and the despised, God has chosen…my message and my preaching were not in persuasive words of wisdom, but in demonstration of the Spirit and of power (1 Corinthians; 1-2).

Endnotes

* **Dr. Vicki Brown** was a visiting professor who taught Cultural Anthropology at Union Biblical Seminary, Pune, at the time of this Consultation.

[1] Seemin Qayum, and Raka Ray, "The Middle Classes at Home," in *Elite and Everyman: The Cultural Politics of the Indian Middle Class*, ed. Amita Baviskar and Raka Ray, 246-270, (New Delhi: Routledge, 2011), 247.

[2] John J. Macionis, *Sociology* (New Jersey: Prentice Hall, 2008), 283.

[3] Macionis, *Sociology*, 284.

[4] Macionis, *Sociology*, 285.

[5] Macionis, *Sociology*, 285.

[6] Carol Upadhya, "Software and the 'New' Middle Class in the 'New India'," in *Elite and Everyman: The Cultural Politics of the Indian Middle Class*, ed. Amita Baviskar and Raka Ray, 167-192, (New Delhi: Routledge, 2011), 181.

[7] Upadhya, "Software and the 'New' Middle Class in the 'New India'," 181-182.

[8] Qayum and Ray, "The Middle Classes at Home," 260.

Bibliography

Macionis, John J. *Sociology*. New Jersey: Prentice Hall, 2008.

New American Standard Bible. Thomas Nelson Publishers, 1977.

Upadhya, Carol. "Software and the 'New' Middle Class in the 'New India'." In *Elite and Everyman: The Cultural Politics of the Indian Middle Class*. Edited by Amita Baviskar and Raka Ray, 167-192. New Delhi: Routledge, 2011.

Qayum, Seemin and Raka Ray. "The Middle Classes at Home." In *Elite and Everyman: The Cultural Politics of the Indian Middle Class*. Edited by Amita Baviskar and Raka Ray, 246-270. New Delhi: Routledge, 2011.

9 789388 945684